Do-It-Yourself
Projects
Gardening Made Easy

Meredith Consumer Marketing
Des Moines, Iowa

Better Homes and Gardens.

Do-It-Yourself
Projects
Gardening Made Easy

MEREDITH CONSUMER MARKETING
Vice President, Consumer Marketing: Janet Donnelly
Consumer Marketing Product Director: Heather Sorensen
Consumer Marketing Product Manager: Wendy Merical
Business Director: Ron Clingman
Senior Production Manager: Al Rodruck

WATERBURY PUBLICATIONS, INC.
Contributing Editor: Karen Weir-Jimerson, Studio G, Inc.
Contributing Copy Editor: Carrie Schmitz
Contributing Proofreader: Gretchen Kauffman
Contributing Indexer: Donald Glassman

Editorial Director: Lisa Kingsley
Creative Director: Ken Carlson
Associate Editors: Tricia Bergman, Mary Williams
Associate Design Director: Doug Samuelson
Production Assistant: Mindy Samuelson

BETTER HOMES AND GARDENS® **MAGAZINE**
Editor in Chief: Gayle Goodson Butler
Managing Editor: Gregory H. Kayko
Creative Director: Michael D. Belknap
Deputy Editor, Gardening: Eric Liskey

MEREDITH NATIONAL MEDIA GROUP
President: Tom Harty

MEREDITH CORPORATION
Chairman and Chief Executive Officer: Stephen M. Lacy

In Memoriam: E.T. Meredith III (1933–2003)

Pictured on the front cover:
top left Preserve flowers from your garden as art. See page 38.
bottom left Make a bubbly fountain for your garden or patio. See page 112.
right Create a cracked-pot succulent garden in just 6 easy steps. See page 68.

Copyright © 2014
Meredith Corporation.
Des Moines, Iowa.
First Edition.
Printed in the United States of America.
ISBN: 978-0-696-30193-3

All of us at Meredith® Consumer Marketing are dedicated to providing you with information and ideas to enhance your home. We welcome your comments and suggestions. Write to us at: Meredith Consumer Marketing, 1716 Locust St., Des Moines, IA 50309-3023.

Contents

Chapter 1

10 GARDEN BASICS
Hands-on projects for beautiful gardens.

Chapter 2

56 HOME AND GARDEN
Garden-inspired decor for inside and out.

Chapter 3

106 WATER WONDERS
Bubbly water-garden projects.

Chapter 4

130 COOL CONTAINERS
Easy plant-by-number container plans.

Chapter 5

154 SUPER STRUCTURES
Beautiful supports for gorgeous plantings.

Chapter 6

178 LANDSCAPE BEAUTIES
Transform your outdoor living spaces.

Easy Does It

Be creative. Grow your own. Save time and money. We'll show you how to enjoy the gardening life with fun and easy projects to enhance your yard and garden.

Living the gardening life—raising vegetables, enjoying flowers, attracting wildlife—is satisfying and fun. Crafting, building, and painting are creative endeavors. Put them together and you have the purpose of this book. For decades, Better Homes and Gardens® has been the leader in do-it-yourself (DIY) projects. This book is packed with artistic and amazing DIY garden projects of every scale—including weekend projects and quick instant-gratification ideas. Have fun!

BEST GARDENING PRACTICES

SAVE TIME

Gather Project Supplies in Advance
When you start a job with the necessary materials at hand, you won't have to interrupt your work to search for items.

Hang Your Tools
Dangling garden tools from hooks makes them readily accessible and helps you keep track of your inventory.

Mulch Beds and Borders
Because mulch smothers weeds and saves water, you'll spend less time weeding and watering your garden. A layer of mulch also makes a tidy base for decorative sculptures and garden accent containers. If you want to keep weeds down, apply mulch in early spring. A 3-inch cover is all you need. Leave a small gap between the mulch and your plant stems or tree trunks.

Use the Right Tool for the Job
A mulch fork is an ideal tool for adding a variety of mulches to your landscape. A mulch fork is an extra-wide, extra-long pitchfork that balances huge scoops of shredded-bark mulch, pine straw, or other chunky mulch to make them feel light and comfortable.

SAVE TIME

Keep Tools Clean
Good garden hygiene can prevent disease transmission. Although gardening is dirty work, it's important to keep your tools clean. Remove soil from spades and trowels and keep pruners clean and well oiled.

Install Edging Around Your Beds
Lawn and garden edging helps keep weeds and grass from growing into beds. Inexpensive edging is available in metal and flexible recycled plastic or rubber. Set flush with ground level, it forms a mowing strip and saves you the work of hand-clipping grass along a taller barrier.

Start Small
If you want a new garden, think small or install it in stages so you can manage the upkeep. New gardens increase your workload because they need frequent weeding and watering until they're established.

Use Raised Beds and Containers
Raised beds and containers let you customize soil and boost your garden's height. Beds should be at least 1 foot deep and no more than 4 feet wide with sides of fieldstone, brick, cinder block, or rot-resistant wood. If kneeling and bending are difficult for you, make the structure wide enough to provide a seat.

SAVE MONEY

Walk Your Garden Daily
When you walk around your garden, check your plants. Do your rhododendrons look yellow? Are Japanese beetles cavorting on the roses? Are your potted plants wilting? Addressing potential problems early helps avoid bigger, more expensive problems in the future.

Make Your Own Mulch
If you have a mulching lawn mower, mow up to a 3-inch layer of leaves and turn it into mulch. If using a riding tractor with a mulching plate and mulching blades, set 4 inches high to chop leaves. After chopping, remove the plate and use the tractor to blow the chopped leaves into beds as needed. Spread the clippings by hand, covering some plants for winter and filling in spots where the mulch level is low.

Divide Perennials
If you need perennials to harmonize with a garden ornament or blend it into the landscape, save yourself a trip to the nursery. You can have new plants for free by lifting and dividing your existing perennials in spring or fall, when root growth is best. Ideally, divide spring and summer bloomers in early to mid-fall and fall-flowering perennials in spring. With extra care, most perennials will survive the process even when your timing's somewhat off.

CHAPTER ONE

Garden Basics

Discover the best ways to do basic gardening techniques: easy potting methods, beautiful bouquets, seed starting, topiaries, and more!

Rosemary Topiary

Many types of plants are well-suited to shaping into little treelike topiaries. Herbs such as rosemary and basil, as well as landscape plants like holly, ivy, and boxwood, make attractive topiaries. Or try flowering plants such as lantana or fuchsia.

Step 1: Establish Roots
Start a rosemary topiary by planting a rooted cutting in a half-and-half mixture of peat moss and perlite. You can also purchase a small rosemary plant at a local nursery or garden center.

Step 2: Pot and Prune
Once the cutting is fully rooted, transplant it to a 3½-inch pot containing sterilized potting soil. Prune the side shoots of the plant to encourage vertical growth.

Step 3: Train the Plant
Stake the plant snugly with twist ties and let it grow in a sunny spot for two months. Water well. When the plant is 2 feet tall, trim off its main vertical shoot. This will stop its upward growth and encourage branching. Strip the bottom two-thirds of the plant of all shoots, leaving the top one-third of its branches for shaping.

TOPIARY CARE

BHG TEST GARDEN TIP

Once the topiary is created, maintaining its treelike shape is easy.

TURN THE PLANT. Plants grow toward the sun, so turn the plant weekly to keep all the foliage the same length.

LOOSEN THE TIES. Keep the trunk of the topiary strong by loosening the ties as it grows. If the ties are too tight, they can girdle the plant.

FEED THE PLANT. Nourish the topiary with a water-soluble fertilizer once a month during summer.

PINCH TO KEEP SHAPE. To keep the rounded topiary shape, pinch off the growing tips.

AVOID ROOT-BOUND PLANTS. Repot the plant or trim the roots to prevent it from becoming root-bound.

opposite Topiaries are classic elements of formal garden design, but they look at home in any type of decor.

Time Required

About 15 minutes

Supplies Needed

Rosemary cutting

Peat moss

Perlite

3½-inch pot

Potting soil

Plant stake

Twist ties, raffia, or jute

Root-Bound Remedy

Any overgrown plant can get a new look by moving it to a bigger pot. Plus some plants will supply smaller plants you can keep or give to friends. Root-bound plants appreciate more space to expand, and you'll have healthier plants.

Time Required

About 15 minutes

Supplies Needed

Gloves
Watering can
Potting soil
Drill with a metal drill bit
New pot
Root-bound plant
Old pot

right A repotted plant is healthier and happier. Some plants, such as aloes, allow you to pull off starts that can be potted and given to friends.

Step 1: Unpot the Plant
Turn the plant upside down to reveal the root system and check to make sure the root network is healthy and has filled the container. If the roots are sparse, you can still do a makeover—just select a container the same size as the original one.

Step 2: Drill Drainage Holes
Find a container that is at least an inch wider than the original pot. Drill at least three drainage holes an inch apart using a metal bit. If you are working with a clay pot, use a masonry bit. (Caution: Drilling holes may damage a container. Don't try this with a valuable one.)

Step 3: Tease Roots Free
Pull the roots from the root ball; this helps them penetrate the new soil. If you want to share the bounty with friends, separate off a "pup" with as many roots as possible. Slip the mother plant into its new container, adding soil around the original root network. Be sure to press the soil around the roots, filling empty holes.

MAKE YOUR OWN POTTING MIX

Use this nutrient-rich blend when planting or replacing plants in containers.

- 8 quarts potting soil with vermiculite or perlite
- 1 quart coarse sand
- 4 quarts sphagnum peat moss, compost, and/or rotted manure

Step 4: Pot the "Pup"
Place the new plant in a pot, tamping down the soil around the roots and giving the division plenty of expansion room to start a new family.

Step 5: Water Well
Keep the roots moderately moist and position the plant out of baking sun for a brief adjustment period. One to two weeks should do it.

Regular repotting, which should
be done after your plant is finished
flowering, ensures that the potting
medium sustains the orchid's needs.

Orchid Potting

Orchids enchant with their ethereal and exotic beauty. To keep them looking their best, repot them every few years. Transfer to a container just large enough to accommodate two years' growth.

Time Required

About 15 minutes

Supplies Needed

Orchid

Potting medium such as bark, gravel, or sphagnum moss

Pot

Razor blade or garden shears

Plastic foam peanuts (if using sphagnum moss)

Step 1: Remove the Plant
Remove the orchid from its container. If you cannot easily remove the plant, gently tap the bottom of the container or slide a sterilized knife around the inside edge of the pot.

Step 2: Discard Dead Roots
Remove the old potting medium from the orchid's roots. Then, using your clean fingernails or a sterilized razor blade, remove the orchid's dead roots. The dead roots are dry, shriveled, and brownish gray. Healthy roots are plump and green. If sphagnum moss is your potting medium, place a few plastic foam peanuts at the bottom of the pot for drainage, then a layer of moss. If you use bark, no drainage material is needed. Position the orchid in the pot and gently insert more potting medium until the roots are covered.

Step 3: Rest in the Shade
Water the orchid lightly and keep it in a shady area for a few days for the plant to recover.

Flower Bouquets

The most beautiful bouquets are not complex. They just take a certain eye for color, shape, texture, and composition. Mix and match flowers. And have some fun!

Time Required

About 15 minutes

Supplies Needed

Cut flowers from the garden or market

A fresh-flower bouquet is a simple and well-appreciated gift because it's always a treat to have fresh flowers in the home. Here are five simple ways to make knockout bouquets for yourself and others.

Idea 1: Use All One Flower

You can never go wrong with carnival-color zinnias. Here, a simple arrangement of zinnias from Benary's Giant Series includes 'Queen Lime', 'Queen Red Lime', and 'Bright Pink'.

Idea 2: Contrast Shapes

Mix spiky flowers such as snapdragon Opus Series 'Appleblossom' or celosia 'Hi Z' with round shapes such as zinnia Benary's Giant Series 'Queen Lime'.

Idea 3: Use Vibrant Colors

Try yellow, red, or orange to make other flowers stand out. Here, lisianthus 'Mariachi Blue' and *Rudbeckia hirta* 'Prairie Sun' combine with *Gomphrena* 'QIS Purple' and cinnamon basil.

Idea 4: Go Subtle

If you want to tone down a bouquet, choose a monochromatic color scheme, as in this combination of dahlia 'Arabian Night' and Karma Sangria, amaranth 'Hot Biscuits', and celosia 'Hi Z'.

Idea 5: Add Fun Fillers

Fillers such as cinnamon basil add green contrast and scent. Try mixing herbs into bouquets, as in this pretty posy of lisianthus 'Pink Champagne', Benary's Giant Series 'Queen Red Lime' zinnia, snapdragon Opus Series 'Appleblossom', celosia 'Hi Z', and cinnamon basil.

Idea 1

BHG TEST GARDEN TIP

BEAUTIFUL BOUQUET TIPS

Create an infinite variety of arrangements using three simple design elements:

FILLER. Start with several stems of filler. They fill in with color and hold blooms in place. Florists often use fern leaves and baby's breath to do this job.

FOCAL POINT. This is the element that makes you go ahh! Often the focal point is the largest bloom with a commanding shape or color. An odd number of these flowers or leaves is the most visually pleasing.

ACCENT. Usually smaller than the focal point, an accent plays a complementary role. Look for a flower or leaf that has a texture, shape, or color different from your filler or your focal point.

Idea 2

Idea 3

Idea 4

Idea 5

19

Grass Place Markers

Make a fresh statement at your next party with an urn sprouting lush green grass at each place setting. Write each person's name on a copper plant marker to make a distinctive tabletop addition. Plus, each guest can take home a sweet little growing gift.

Time Required

About 15 minutes

Supplies Needed

One 5-inch-tall cast-iron urn per person (available at garden centers)

Potting soil

Grass seed, any variety (1 cup of seed is enough for six place markers)

Spray bottle

Copper plant markers

Medium-tip permanent marking pen

Step 1: Prepare the Urns

Fill each urn with potting soil to about ½ inch from the rim to give the seeds enough growing room. Use potting soil, not dirt from your yard. Potting soil is lighter and will allow the grass to germinate faster.

Step 2: Sow the Grass Seeds

Sprinkle enough seeds to cover the top of the soil. Press the seeds gently into the soil or cover with a thin layer of soil. Using a spray bottle, water well. Write each person's name on a copper plant marker using a permanent marking pen. Gently push each plant marker into a grass-filled urn.

opposite If you're planning a dinner party or other event, plant the grass seeds about two weeks ahead so the grass has time to grow tall enough.

Moss Centerpiece

Foam spheres covered with moss make a simple and elegant tabletop centerpiece. And they are so easy! Arranged in a group on a side or dining table, they make a sophisticated statement. Vary the size of your spheres to add interest.

Time Required

About 15 minutes

Supplies Needed

One 7-inch-tall cast-iron urn

Three or four plastic-foam spheres (combination of 3-, 4-, 6-, and 8-inch spheres)

1 package light reindeer moss

1 package dark reindeer moss

Several pieces of sheet moss (available at crafts stores)

Hot-glue gun

Old cotton cloth (to protect your hands from burns while pressing moss onto spheres)

Bowl of ice water

Scissors

Spray bottle

Green food coloring

Step 1: Make Moss Balls

Use a hot-glue gun to apply glue to the back of a small piece of light reindeer moss. The size of the piece depends on the sphere size; you want the result to be a patchwork of different-tone mosses. Because reindeer moss is pricier than sheet moss, use it sparingly. Press moss firmly onto the sphere, using a cotton cloth to protect your hands and arms from burns. Keep a bowl of ice water handy in case of any mishaps. Repeat the process using a small piece of dark reindeer moss, then again with a larger piece of sheet moss.

Step 2: Patch and Trim

Continue to apply alternating types of reindeer and sheet moss until the sphere is covered with an even patchwork. Trim loose pieces with scissors. Repeat with other spheres; place an appropriate-size sphere gently atop the urn. Keep the spheres out of direct sunlight and spritz them occasionally using a spray bottle that contains water and six drops of green food coloring.

opposite Moss hot-glued to plastic-foam spheres takes on life when spritzed with water.

Bird-Feeding Urn

Thrill your backyard buddies with a sphere rolled in their favorite birdseed. Place the seed-covered globe in an urn on a patio table or within view from a window and watch the party begin.

Time Required

About 15 minutes

Supplies Needed

Two bags of birdseed (one each of black sunflower seeds and a birdseed mix)

Rectangular pan or tray with sides, such as a jelly-roll pan or disposable plastic-foam tray

Plastic-foam spheres (6- and 8-inch spheres for urn toppers; 3- and 4-inch for tabletop spheres)

Butter knife or frosting spatula

Tree branch or chopstick

Creamy peanut butter

Waxed paper

One 10-inch-tall cast-iron urn

One 8-inch-tall cast-iron urn

Step 1: Spread Peanut Butter
Fill pan with enough seed to evenly cover the bottom. Place a plastic-foam sphere in the birdseed-filled pan (or on another protected surface). Using a butter knife or frosting spatula, smoothly spread peanut butter onto the sphere until it's covered. To make the job easier, insert a chopstick or tree branch into the sphere to use as a handle to turn the sphere as you spread the peanut butter.

Step 2: Roll in Birdseed
When the sphere is covered in peanut butter, roll it in the seed-filled pan. Use your hands to press the birdseed firmly into place. Continue rolling, as needed, until the entire surface is covered. Place the spheres on trays lined with waxed paper. Refrigerate for six to eight hours or until set. Remove the spheres from the refrigerator; set the large ones on the urns. Place the urns and small spheres on an outdoor tabletop or in your garden.

opposite Plastic-foam spheres covered with peanut butter and birdseed make attractive tabletop feeders and pose no danger to birds. When you see the foam showing through, apply another layer of peanut butter and seed.

Seed Starting

The techniques and materials involved in planting seeds are simple and few, but the rewards are many. Growing plants from seed is economical and fun. Here's what you need to know for success.

If you're not drawn in by the practical benefits of starting plants from seed—saving money, getting a head start on the growing season, and choosing from an incredible selection of varieties beyond what's available in flats at the nursery—then consider the sheer joy and wonder of the process. Magic and mystery await in watching a seemingly lifeless seed sprout into a living, growing plant, and the miracle of this transformation carries with it a sense of hope.

The two main types of seeds are hybrid and heirloom. Hybrid seeds (designated by F1 or F2 on the package) are formed by cross-fertilizing two plant varieties to achieve certain desirable traits, such as disease resistance or high yield. Be warned: If you save and grow seeds from a hybrid, your seedlings will not grow true to the parent plant; they will be throwbacks to other varieties used in the hybridization—or they may not germinate.

Heirloom seeds come from open-pollinated plant varieties—those fertilized naturally by wind, water, insects, or birds. Sowing heirloom seeds gives a sense of history; some varieties date to the 1800s. Once in danger of phasing out, heirloom seeds are now more readily available.

Starting Times

Knowing when to start seeds indoors takes some backward thinking. First, find the average date of the last frost in your area and the number of weeks before that date you should start a particular kind of seed. (The number of weeks varies from plant to plant and is typically listed on the seed package.) Then count backward on the calendar from the average last frost date. Most seeds should be started six to eight weeks before the last frost date. Some seeds can be started just a couple of weeks before it, while others may need a lead time of 12–14 weeks. Starting seeds in March or even February can lift your spirits. But don't get carried away. If you start seeds too early, you'll have to keep the seedlings inside too long, and they may be weak and spindly by the time the weather is right for planting outside.

Gather Your Gear

The containers you choose as homes for your seeds need not be fancy. A beautiful plant can begin life in the humblest surroundings. A cardboard egg carton makes an excellent seed-starting flat, as do cut-down milk cartons or jugs, yogurt cups, nursery flats, foam take-out containers, and disposable aluminum pans. Biodegradable peat pots also work well. Whatever you choose, make sure the container has proper drainage holes.

opposite Seeds sown in biodegradable pots can be planted directly into the ground.

 EASY COSMOS

A must-have annual for sunny cottage gardens, cosmos offers ferny foliage and daisylike flowers in shades of pink, magenta, white, yellow, and orange. The plants don't mind hot, dry locations, so they're ideal for low-maintenance gardens, too. And they often self-seed. Spread seeds over the ground and just barely cover them; seeds usually sprout in one to three weeks.

Seed Starting

Time Required

About 15 minutes

Supplies Needed

Seeds

Planting containers for seeds, such as a cardboard egg cartons, yogurt cups, or trimmed milk cartons

Commercial seed-starting mixture

Pencil (use the eraser tip to push seeds down to the desired depth)

Plant labels

Step 1: Plant Your Seeds

Seeds contain enough food to support the germinating seedlings in their first days. Start them in a sterile, weed-free mixture that holds water but is not so densely packed that it keeps air out and inhibits roots. Many good commercial seed-starting mixtures are available. Most contain some combination of vermiculite, sphagnum moss, and perlite. Do not use ordinary garden soil; it's too heavy for delicate seedlings and may also carry fungi, toxins, or pests. Many seedlings look alike, so labels are a good idea. Write the plant names on wood crafts sticks or other labels and stick them in the soil.

Step 2: Get Growing

Add water. It's important to keep your seed-starting medium moist—but not soggy—until sprouts appear. Small containers can dry out quickly, so check them often. Cover the containers with a clear plastic lid or bag to preserve moisture, but leave an opening for air to circulate. Seeds vary in the amount of light they need to germinate; some require light, and others germinate best in darkness. Seeds should be covered with ¼ inch of fine soil, firmed down. Check seed packets for recommendations.

Step 3: Nurture Seedlings

After germination, light is essential. It can be either natural or artificial. Seedlings require 12–16 hours of light every day. The recommended soil temperature range for most seeds started indoors is 75°F–90°F. Place seed-starting containers in a warm spot, such as near a heat vent, near a kitchen range, or on top of the refrigerator. A soil-heating cable or electric heating mat can also keep the growing medium warm. After the seedlings are up, warmth is not as critical. A range of 60°F–70°F is fine. In fact, some gardeners believe seedlings will grow stronger and healthier if allowed to cool down 5–10 degrees at night.

Step 4: Thin Your Plants

As seedlings develop their first set of true leaves (after the initial seed leaves), the containers will become crowded, and you'll need to do some thinning. It goes against instincts to get rid of healthy plants, but if you let the crowding continue, all the plants will suffer. Keep the largest, healthiest seedlings; cut off the stems of the unwanted plants at soil level or share the extra seedlings with friends. Leave at least an inch of space between the remaining seedlings. As the survivors grow and outdoor temperatures reach at least 50°F, the seedlings are ready to harden off (get tough) by being set in a protected area outdoors, such as a greenhouse, garage, or cold frame. After a day or two, they will be ready to move to the garden.

Step 5: Troubleshoot

Most seeds are fairly forgiving of variances in growing conditions, but things can go wrong.

Damping off is a condition when seedlings suddenly wilt and die. This is caused by fungi. Avoid overwatering. Thin seedlings to prevent crowding. Use a sterile growing medium, make sure all containers are clean, and mist seeds with a soluble fungicide after sowing.

Leggy plants—those that become long and spindly—may be receiving too little light, growing in overly warm conditions, or overcrowded.

Discolored leaves may occur if there is a nutrient deficiency. Solve this problem with a weekly dose of a liquid fertilizer at half-strength.

Hanging Basket

Follow these simple steps to create a customized basket of blooms. When you plant your own hanging baskets, you can use the colors and plants you like best. Plus, you can plant larger, more mature plants to get a lush look.

Time Required

About 15 minutes

Supplies Needed

Wire or plastic basket

Coconut coir or sphagnum liner

Trowel

Potting soil

Slow-release fertilizer

Flowering trailing annual plants such as calibrachoa, bidens, or Supertunias

Water

right A hanging basket packed with blue calibrachoa and yellow bidens makes a cheery addition to any front porch or patio.

Step 1: Gather Materials
Assemble your materials on a potting bench or outdoor table. Potting can be messy, so it's best to do it outdoors.

Step 2: Place Liner in Basket
With your hands or a trowel, fill the basket about halfway with damp potting soil mix. If the soil does not contain fertilizer, add three to four handfuls per 20-inch width.

Step 3: Dig In
With a trowel, make a hole for each plant so the soil level will barely cover the root ball. Flip plants upside down and gently tap to free them from their pots.

Step 4: Tuck In the Plants
If the root ball is tight, make four or more vertical cuts in the ball about ½ inch deep to encourage new growth. Place the plants inside the holes.

Step 5: Pat Down
Firm each plant into the potting soil mix with your hands, adding soil around it. If necessary, add more soil to within ½ inch of the rim of the basket.

Step 6: Water Well
Add water until it drips through the basket. Water again to ensure the soil is thoroughly wet. Let any excess water drain out of the planter, then hang it.

Drip Irrigation

Consumer-friendly do-it-yourself irrigation systems make watering chores faster. Drip systems will also help you save money because this watering method is the most efficient way to keep plants healthy and hydrated.

Few gardeners look forward to watering their plants, especially after a long day of work. But it doesn't have to be a dreaded chore. With a little initial effort and investment, watering tasks can become a breeze.

With many modern gardeners concerned about the environment, the phrase "drip irrigation" has achieved buzzword status in the past decade. Drip systems use up to 70 percent less water than conventional sprinklers.

Pinpointing water directly at the base of plants means less water is lost to evaporation, as occurs with overhead sprinklers that blow water through the air and force it to seep through mulch. Also, with drip irrigation, no water is wasted on unplanted patches, which only encourages weeds. And because drippers apply water with little force, there is less runoff.

Directing water into the ground and not onto leaves may also help save the lives of many plants, especially roses, Mediterranean plants, alpines, and other perennials and annuals that are susceptible to mildew, black spot, fusarium wilt, rust, and other waterborne diseases. Many diseases are spread when water splashes from the ground to the lower limbs or from leaf to leaf.

A seldom-considered advantage of drip irrigation is its unobtrusiveness. Most systems work best when covered with mulch to slow evaporation. Drip-irrigation systems have other unsung benefits. They are compatible with the water pressure in most homes, which means you can shower while the system runs without worrying how to get the shampoo out of your hair.

A drip system can be as simple as a soaker hose or a pipe with holes punched in it, but these methods tend to lose pressure as water moves through the line, so plants closest to the source get too much water and those farthest away die of thirst. The problem is worse if you run a hose uphill. With most modern drip-irrigation systems, however, the dripper heads regulate the water pressure so the plants get an even distribution all along the line. Some systems even deliver fertilizer via an applicator at the beginning of the line. That's one less maintenance worry. The main limitation of drip-irrigation systems is that they are designed mainly for plants in beds, borders, and containers—not lawns.

Although many developments have been made in the selection of heads, antisiphon valves, pressure regulators, and other complex parts, the beauty of drip irrigation lies in its simplicity. In terms of cost and ease of installation, it's not all that far removed from the ordinary garden hose. In fact, you might find it so agreeable, you'll be tempted to dig up your entire front lawn and convert it into a series of giant flowerbeds.

EFFICIENT DELIVERY
The keen ability of drip irrigation to place moisture near these individual cosmos and yarrow plants means little water is wasted on evaporation, bare ground, or unwanted weeds. Less water on the foliage means longer blossoms and a decreased incidence of disease.

opposite Overhead drip systems can regularly water hanging baskets and window boxes that are out of reach with a watering can.

Drip Irrigation

Time Required

1 to 2 hours

Supplies Needed

Drip system kit (available at nurseries and garden centers) that includes ¼-inch vinyl tubing, clamps, ½-inch plastic tubing, ¾-inch adapters, dripper heads, hole punch, elbow joints, antisiphon valve (optional), and battery-operated timer

Step 1: Get Started

After you've completed your irrigation plan, hook up the ½-inch plastic tubing to the ¾-inch adapter, which also serves as a pressure regulator. This adapter screws onto the antisiphon valve required by health codes to prevent backflow of impurities. The antisiphon valve can be hooked to a timer to make the entire system self-sufficient.

Step 2: Lay the Lines

Wind the ½-inch plastic tubing through the area you want to irrigate. One helpful hint: Leave the hose in the sun for about an hour before beginning. This will relax some of the hose's tightly wound memory and make it easier to conform to your beds. At the end of the line, crimp the tubing and secure it with the clamps provided. In this installation, we also used an elbow joint to extend the hose around the corner of the deck. The elbow slips onto two sections of the hose as a splice. No tape or glue is necessary. If you opt to simply curve the hose, be sure to make a wide turn to prevent crimps in the tubing.

Step 3: Link Your Lines

Use a hole punch (included in the kit) to make an opening for the ¼-inch adapter. One end of the barbed adapter fits into the hole, and the other end slips snugly into a short length of ¼-inch flexible vinyl tubing. Before cutting a section of the tubing, set up your container where you want it and measure the distance from the top of the pot to the ½-inch tubing. Remember to measure twice and cut once.

Step 4: Tube Your Pots

Run the ¼-inch vinyl tubing up through a hole in the bottom of your container and attach a head. A bubbler works well for large pots because it will give a slightly wider distribution of water than a regular dripper to ensure that all of the plants receive water. Set the head on the rim and fill the container with potting soil and plants. Position your dripper head so all of the plants will receive water.

Step 5: Final Touches

Set your finished container on feet to prevent the flexible vinyl tubing from being pinched under the weight of the pot. If your containers are on a deck with wide gaps between the boards, you might be able to run the tubing through the cracks and forgo the pot feet. If you want to add a drip system to an existing planted container, run the tubing on the outside of the pot. Uncrimp the end of the ½-inch plastic tubing and briefly turn on the spigot to flush out any debris that might have gotten into the system during installation. Occasionally check your pots for pests, disease, and fertilizer needs.

Growing Greens

Choose from hundreds of varieties of quick-growing edible (and ornamental!) lettuces to pot up in containers alone, with other veggies, or even mixed with flowers. Enjoy a salad bar in your own backyard.

Time Required

1 to 2 hours

Supplies Needed

Four planting containers at least 8×24 inches, such as a wooden box or a galvanized tub

Assortment of loose-leaf lettuces

Organic fertilizer

Plant colorful lettuces in playful designs and harvest a continuous feast for the palate and eye.

Use any type of container to create a garden salad bar. Wood boxes, whiskey half barrels, and old enamelware come to life with tender greens; wheelbarrows and coaster wagons create veritable meals on wheels.

Stick with loose-leaf lettuces, which mature in about 45 days. It's harder to control aesthetics if you're mixing in head lettuces, too.

Step 1: Select Containers
Choose four containers, each at least 8×24 inches, to rotate the timing of your plantings. Make drainage holes in all and fill containers with potting soil.

Step 2: Sow Seeds
Sprinkle seeds into the first container. Lightly water.

Step 3: Harvest Lettuces and Plant Next Container
When lettuce seedlings are 1 inch tall (after seven to 10 days), plant the next container. Repeat the process. Cut lettuces will grow back three or four times, but you'll reap the best flavor if you pick the entire plant once, then replant.

Step 4: Add Fertilizer
Fertilize with an organic mix of fish emulsion and liquid seaweed.

BHG TEST GARDEN TIP — PRETTY PAIRS

Try these lettuce companions.

'Merlot' (deep burgundy) and 'Black-Seeded Simpson' (light green).

'Valeria' (intense red) and 'Bolzano' (pale green). Both have frilly edges.

'Maserati' (red) and 'Smile' (green). Both are compact, medium-size oak-leaf lettuces.

'Salad Bowl' (green) and 'Red Salad Bowl' (red).

Greens aren't just green; they are also red and speckled. Try a delicious and attractive mix of different types of loose-leaf lettuces for salads and sautés.

Flower Pressing

Enjoy flowers and foliage from your garden forever. Create pressed-flower garden collages, then hang them on your porch or inside your home. Make hanging artwork by season and switch them out whenever it suits you.

Time Required

1 to 2 hours

Supplies Needed

Flowers and herbs

Flower press

Scrapbooking paper

12×12-inch foam square

Decoupage medium

Paint brushes

Step 1: Press Flowers
Begin by pressing flowers, herbs, leaves, buds, and leaves in a book or a microwave flower press, as shown here. Lay one to three plant parts on the press, cover with a piece of linen (provided in the kit), and clamp tight.

Step 2: Microwave the Press
Microwave the press according to instructions provided with the flower-press kit. You may need to experiment by trial and error to determine the proper times for your microwave oven.

Step 3: Remove Pressed Blooms
Carefully remove the press from the microwave, open the top, and remove the pressed plant parts. Set aside.

Step 4: Add Background to Foam
Choose 12×12-inch scrapbooking papers (available at hobby retailers) to coordinate with pressed flowers and leaves. Brush decoupage medium onto back of paper, then press over a 12×12-inch foam square. The paper should lie flat as it dries.

Step 5: Decoupage the Flower
After the paper has dried in place, begin brushing decoupage medium onto the square, then gently lay the pressed flowers and leaves over the medium. Press down gently with a brush or your fingertips. This is a delicate process, but it's easy to master.

Step 6: Seal and Display
Once all plant parts are in place, seal with one to three layers of decoupage medium. Finish the piece by gluing decorative ribbon around the edges of the foam square, then add mounting hardware to the back of the square.

Forcing Branches

Bring dormant branches of flowering trees, such as crabapples and forsythia, indoors so you can enjoy spring early. A little warm air and water will "force" the branches into beautiful bloom.

Time Required

1 to 2 hours

Supplies Needed

Dormant flowering branches
Pruner
Utility knife
Water
Vase

right Freshly forced crabapple branches make a beautiful spring centerpiece.

Step 1: Cut Dormant Branches
Select pencil-thick branch sections 12–24 inches long that boast numerous plump buds. Using a sharp knife or hand pruner, cut the branch, making an angled cut at the base. Immediately place each branch in water.

Step 2: Strip and Pare
Bring the branches inside, then strip buds, twigs, and leaves from lower sections that will be underwater. Use a utility knife to pare away an inch or two of bark from the base. Smash woody bases with a hammer. These openings enhance water absorption.

Step 3: Hydrate the Branches
Place branches in a water-filled container set in a bathtub and give them a long, tepid shower. Wrap branches in wet newspaper, then place them in clean, lukewarm water. Move to a cool, dark spot; mist branches and change water daily. Unwrap after two or three days.

Step 4: Place Flowers in a Vase
Once the flowers start to pop, arrange branches in a tall, water-filled vase or pitcher and bring them into the spotlight. Set the arrangement in a bright-but-cool spot out of direct sunlight. The cooler the spot, the longer the branches will bloom.

BHG TEST GARDEN TIP

BRANCHES BY THE MONTH

Bring branches to force into bloom indoors for each month leading into spring.

JANUARY Depending on where you live and what you plant, you can start hauling in armloads of Cornelian cherry dogwood (*Cornus mas*), forsythia, vernal witch hazel (*Hamamelis vernalis*), and pear tree branches as early as January.

FEBRUARY Gather branches from flowering quince (*Chaenomeles* spp., pictured), rhododendron, pussy willow (*Salix discolor*), apple and crabapple (*Malus* spp.) trees, and cherry (*Prunus* spp.) trees.

MARCH Continue the chain of soul-lifting spring color with March-clipped boughs of magnolias, mountain laurel (*Kalmia latifolia*), beautybush (*Kolkwitzia amabilis*), lilacs, flowering dogwood (*Cornus florida*), mock orange (*Philadelphus* spp.), bridalwreath (*Spiraea prunifolia*), deutzia, and fothergilla.

Stepping-Stones

Sure, you can wheel into the home center and grab from the pallet of mass-produced stepping-stones. But with a little effort—and planning ahead—you can create your own works of art.

Time Required

1 to 2 days

Supplies Needed

Oil-base modeling clay

Pencil and paper

Sharp knife

Plywood work board

Nonstick cooking spray

Model latex (available at art supply stores)

Paintbrush

Pot for boiling water

4–6 feet of 1×3 pine boards

Wood screws and screwdriver

Masonite board

Concrete mix

Chicken wire

Brick fragment (for sanding edges)

Latex paint (if desired)

right Concrete stepping-stones are personalized garden ornaments and make great gifts for garden-loving friends and family.

Step 1: Play with Clay
Press oil-base modeling clay into a ¼-inch-thick slab. Draw a pattern on paper and place it on the clay. Cut around the pattern with a knife. Place the clay pieces on an uncut copy of the paper pattern glued to a plywood board. Sculpt a model by shaping and joining clay pieces. Spritz with nonstick cooking spray.

Step 2: Cover with Latex
Brush a thin layer of model latex over the surface of the clay model. Apply slowly to prevent air bubbles. Allow to dry about 10 minutes (check label for directions). Repeat the process until the mold is ¼ inch thick (20–25 coats). Allow to dry completely overnight. Remove the mold from the clay model and boil it for 10 minutes to strengthen the latex.

Step 3: Build a Box
Make a shallow square box to hold the rubber mold. For the box frame, use 1×3-inch pine furring strips cut to the size of the mold and secure strips with screws. Use a square of Masonite for the bottom of the box. Insert the rubber mold, design side up, in the box.

Step 4: Mix Concrete
Prepare ready-mix concrete following package directions. A 60-pound bag makes four 14-inch square stepping-stones.

Step 5: Pour Concrete
Scoop enough concrete into the box to cover the design (about 1 inch thick). Place a piece of chicken wire, cut smaller than the mold, over the concrete for reinforcement. Continue pouring concrete until the box is filled. Smooth the surface with a trowel and tap the box on the work surface to remove air bubbles. Allow the concrete to set for 24 hours out of direct sunlight.

Step 6: Remove the Stone
Loosen the screws, invert the box, and gently tap it to release the stone onto a cushioned surface. Gently remove the latex mold from the stone. (If the stone is left in the mold longer than 24 hours, it will be more difficult to remove and the mold may tear.)

Step 7: Sand It Smooth
Use a brick to smooth rough edges and remove imperfections. Allow the stone to cure for one week.

Step 8: Add Color
To color a stone, dip it in a bucket filled with a mixture of equal parts exterior latex paint and water. Or use a large paintbrush to apply the diluted paint onto all sides of the stone. Allow it to dry for about one hour.

MOSAIC STONES

To create mosaic stones, make a leaf, circle, square, or other shape stone from concrete. Leave a depressed area to fill later with stone or glass pieces set in mortar. Make sure they are level; pieces that stick up will break off.

SHELLS OR STONES Embellish stepping-stones with natural found objects such as shells and stones. Press them into the concrete to make them level with the surface.

CERAMIC OR TILE Use broken shards of ceramic or tiles to decorate the surface of the stepping-stones. Use a color motif that matches your garden or patio furnishings.

Cast Leaves

Hard as rock, concrete ornaments are easy to make. Even better, this versatile outdoor material is low-cost. Enhance your garden with leaf-shape stepping-stones. Use large leaves, such as rhubarb, as a guide for sculpting stones for a sure-footed path through the garden.

Time Required

2 to 4 hours

Supplies Needed

Large leaves, such as rhubarb
Pea gravel
Quick-setting concrete
Water
Tray
Trowel

Step 1: Plan Spacing
Start by planning a path of staggered steps matching your stride. Carve each leaf-shape hole about 3 inches deep.

Step 2: Add Gravel
Lay a 1-inch drainable base of pea gravel topped by ½ inch of coarse sand into each hole.

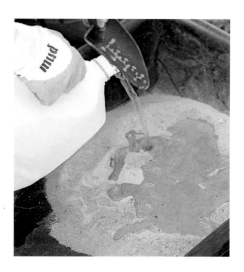

Step 3: Make the Concrete
Prepare the concrete, adding water slowly to half a bag of quick-setting mix (choose one that starts hardening in about 15 minutes).

BHG TEST GARDEN TIP

CONCRETE BIRD BASIN

A simple basin settles easily into the garden's edge, where feathered friends can drop in to drink, splash, and bathe. Form your birdbath in the garden by scooping out a shallow hole, shaping a 15-inch-wide and 3-inch-deep mold in the soil. Press bits of tumbled recycled glass into the surface of the still-wet concrete for a touch of sparkle.

Step 4: Stir the Concrete
Blend the concrete with a hand trowel until it is thoroughly moist and resembles chunky peanut butter.

Step 5: Fill the Hole
Fill the hole evenly with concrete. Use your hands to press and sculpt the concrete into a leaf shape.

Step 6: Apply the Leaf
Place a rhubarb leaf, vein side down, on the surface of the concrete. Press firmly to make a detailed impression. Lift off the leaf.

Step 7: Enhance the Veins
Deepen the veins of the leaf using a wooden skewer.

Step 8: Cover and Cure
Cover the stepping-stone with damp burlap. Keep it covered and damp to help strengthen the concrete while it cures for a week.

Wind Chimes

Create inexpensive wind chimes from recycled empty wine or water bottles. The bottles catch light and softly clink together in the wind.

Time Required
1 to 2 hours

Supplies Needed
Wine bottles
Aluminum wire

Step 1: Assemble Bottles
Wash and dry four to six bottles in different colors.

Step 2: Wrap Necks with Wire
Cut a length of wire appropriate to the drop length of the hanging bottles. Add several inches extra to wrap the bottle neck.

Step 3: Hang Bottles
Hang the bottles at varying heights from a pergola or other overhead structure.

Gently clinking wine bottles in different colors make easy and attractive wind chimes.

BHG TEST GARDEN TIP

RECYCLED BOTTLE EDGING

Edge your landscape in colored-glass bottles to infuse your yard with a funky, down-home look. Bury the bottles neck down, side by side in the soil, to use as garden edging. To keep turf or weeds from migrating from your lawn into your beds, sink a sheet of aluminum flashing about 8 inches into the ground alongside the bottles.

Vine Trellis in a Pot

Morning glories intertwined with golden hops vine makes a gorgeous focal point in a garden. Or plant a pair of them to flank the doorway to a garden. Both vines are fast-growing. The morning glories will flower all summer up until frost.

Time Required

1 to 2 hours

Supplies Needed

Terra-cotta pot
White oil-base paint diluted with paint thinner
Rubber gloves
Rag
2 wire coat hangers
Purchased potting soil
2 conical tomato cages (green or silver)
Pliers
2 golden hops plants
2 blue morning glory seedlings
Small topiary wire form to use as a finial (optional)

right Morning glories are vigorous annual vines that really take off in hot weather. They will bloom until frost.

Step 1: Age the Pot
Wearing gloves, apply white paint diluted to a milky consistency to the entire exterior of the pot using a rag. Rub it in like you're polishing a car; use inconsistent strokes for a mottled effect. Repeat the process once more on the pot rim.

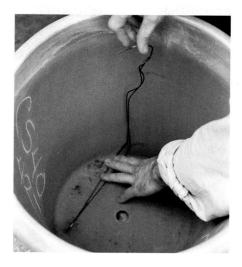

Step 2: Insert Hangers
Bend both coat hangers into L shapes; place in pot, leaving hook even with the eventual level of the soil. Fill the pot with potting soil.

Step 3: Create Climbing Structure
Position one cage directly over the other. Hold top cage and make a quarter turn. (Using two cages instead of one makes a tighter grid for the plants to climb.) If desired, secure the small topiary form as the finial at the top of the tomato cages using small-gauge wire or twine.

Step 4: Plant Hops Vine
Plant the golden hops vine in the center of the container.

Step 5: Insert the Structure
Place the cages, wide ends down, in pot, catching the coat-hanger hooks. Hook the cage in place. Use pliers to squeeze hooks shut over cage frame, pushing frame into soil.

Step 6: Plant the Morning Glories
Reach through the bottom of the cage and insert morning glory vine seedlings into the soil on each side of the planter. Wind plants around the cage so foliage fills in at the bottom before moving up. Water daily in the summer.

Scarecrow

Make your own customized scarecrow. It's a fun afternoon project for kids or a group of friends. Scarecrows are traditional garden sentries, meant to scare off birds from eating crops. Yours can be a friendly addition to a small vegetable or flower garden.

Time Required

6 to 8 hours

Supplies Needed

THE FRAME

2×4s (two 8-foot lengths)
Wooden dowel or broomstick
Eye hook
Length of rebar
3-inch screws
Drill

THE BODY PARTS

Head: grapevine ball
Head stuffing: raffia or Spanish moss
Hair: asparagus fern
Facial features: felt, pinecones, seashells, or other natural decorations
Body stuffing: plastic bags, aluminum cans, straw

THE CONNECTORS

Glue gun
Stapler

THE OUTFIT

Jeans
Shirt
Shoes or boots

opposite A scarecrow doesn't have to be scary. This lovely garden lady, *right,* sports a broad smile and a string of beads. Her asparagus fern hair never needs combing. The scarecrow, *left,* uses a birdhouse for a head.

Step 1: Measure for Lumber
Measure the waist and the length of the jeans as well as the length of the shirt from shoulder to hem. Cut the lumber to suit these measurements. Cut 2×4s legs slightly shorter than the length of the jeans.

NOTE: The scarecrow's torso is made with four pieces of wood: one for the hips, two upright pieces for the chest, and a short piece in between the parallel upright pieces. The scarecrow's torso (the upright pieces) should be slightly shorter than distance between the shirt's collar and hem (if it is a straight hem). The horizontal piece for the hips should be cut to fit inside the waistband of the pants. The shorter horizontal piece at the top supports the scarecrow's neck and head; drill a hole through the center big enough to accommodate the dowel.

Step 2: Start with the Torso
Use a couple of screws to attach the upright torso pieces to the short piece that supports the neck. Screw the hips to the torso. Screw the hips down onto the legs.

Step 3: Make a Horseshoe Shape
When the frame for the scarecrow is complete, it looks like two horseshoe-shape forms screwed together, with the smaller one on top.

Step 4: Attach an Eye Hook
With a countersinking bit, drill a shallow hole in the top of the scarecrow's hips to provide a footing for the dowel. Attach a sturdy eye hook to the hip section of the frame.

Step 5: Put On Jeans and Shoes
With the frame flat on the ground, pull the jeans onto the 2×4 legs and then put the shoes on the bottom of the 2×4s. Drive a screw up through each shoe sole into the 2×4 so the shoes don't fall off.

Step 6: Stand the Frame Up
The jeans should fit around the scarecrow's waist, with the eye hook sticking out the back right about the waistline.

Step 7: Position Rebar
Hammer a rebar rod into the ground and thread the eye hook over the rebar. Zip up the pants; they should fit snugly around the frame so they won't fall down. You can tighten them with a piece of twine or a belt if they're too big at the waist.

Step 8: Build the Head
Secure the grapevine ball to the dowel with a nail at the top. You need a hole in the ball so you can stuff the head with Spanish moss. Clip an opening with pruning shears. The Spanish moss creates a backdrop for the scarecrow's features.

Step 9: Make Fern Hair
Divide a potted asparagus fern into small sections.

Step 10: Bag the Roots
Wrap each clump of fern roots in a resealable sandwich bag. The plastic bag holds the soil and retains moisture.

Step 11: Insert the Hair
Stuff each bag of ferns into the scarecrow's head, teasing the ferny foliage out through the grapevine mesh. To keep the fern foliage fresh, you can simply mist the scarecrow's head. Ornamental grasses also make good hair. If your scarecrow wears a hat, hair may not be necessary.

Step 12: Make Facial Features
The scarecrow's features can be made with pinecones, seashells, bits of bark, wire moss, and marbles or gemstones (available at hobby shops), all secured to the grapevine-ball head with hot glue. The big smile is made of wire moss.

Step 13: Dress the Torso
Put the shirt on the top part of the frame. Stuff the arms and torso with plastic bags to fill them out.

Step 14: Top with the Head
Insert the dowel into the torso.

Step 15: Add Hands
If you want, make moss hands or attach moss-filled garden gloves.

CHAPTER TWO

Home and Garden

Enjoy garden-inspired projects that add color and whimsy to your indoor and outdoor spaces.

Indian Corn Chic

Recruit a vintage rake and some ears of colorful Indian corn into service as a late-season outdoor decoration. The dried ears will last through autumn and look good even after the snow flies.

Fall is a fleeting season, yet it supplies abundant materials for decorating outdoors. To make the most of this time, cull the garden for ingredients to fashion this quick and easy display of nature's bounty. If you grow this corn in your garden, wait until the husks are no longer green before picking. The ears may be one color, such as russet or yellow. Some ears may sport multicolor kernel colors including white, yellow, burgundy, blue, and black. There are oversize and mini ears for a variety of decorating needs.

Time Required
About 15 minutes

Supplies Needed
Vintage garden fork or rake

Assorted ears of colorful Indian corn

Wire

Idea 1: Pitchfork Garnish
Gather dried ears of Indian corn from a farm stand or your garden. Pull back the husks, then wire the ears to a pitchfork for a colorful autumn sentry.

Idea 2: Rake Revise
Use colorful Indian corn ears on an old rake to make a country-style door decoration. Wire the ears to the tines of the rake.

opposite Indian corn captures all the colors of autumn in its colorful kernels. Tease up the paperlike husks for added appeal. Add pumpkins and gourds to complete the garden-inspired decor.

Silly Stakes

Make colorful decorative garden stakes to add whimsy to garden beds and borders.

Time Required

About 15 minutes

Supplies Needed

Project 1 (*opposite*)

Terra-cotta pot

Large wood beads

Twist of copper wire strung with beads and stuck in a cork

Drawer knob

Watering can-shape refrigerator magnet

Wood pinwheel (decorated with acrylic paint)

Plastic Christmas ornament

Project 2 (*top right*)

Plastic foam ball

Twist of copper wire strung with beads and stuck in a cork

Bouncy ball

Plastic foam ball

Fishing bobber

Large wood beads

Project 3 (*bottom right*)

Large glass marble

Aluminum pot (planted with violas)

Glass doorknob

Cedar finial

Brass doorknob

Dress up your garden! These decorative topped garden stakes are fun and useful. Set the stakes in the garden to help support tall, floppy garden beauties such as delphinium or hollyhock. Or create a trio and secure the tops together to make a tepee for vines such as morning glories. You can even dress up a tomato cage.

Decorative stake toppers are hiding in household drawers and workshop corners. Copper wire, beads, repurposed refrigerator magnets, doorknobs, drawer pulls, old Christmas ornaments, and any other interesting trinkets make fun tops. Suitable staking materials include bamboo sticks, wood dowels, copper pipe, plastic pipe, broom handles, reinforcing rod, and plastic-covered steel.

Step 1: Assemble Materials
Make several stakes at once.

Step 2: Connect Stake and Top
Use a nail, screw, or epoxy glue to attach each top to a stake.

Step 3: Decorate Your Garden
Set stakes in a flowerbed, along a walkway, or in a large container.

above right You can find decorative toppers anywhere in the house, garage, garden shed, or kids' playbox.
right Cluster stakes in a garden as a colorful focal point.
opposite Toppers can include small pots planted with tiny flowers such as violas.

Etched Glass Vase

Transform any clear-glass bottle or jar into a beautiful etched vase. Simple crafts store supplies (etching cream and adhesive shelf liner) add lacy, frosty frills to plain glass. Create your own custom vases for holiday gifts or as single-bouquet place settings for a garden party. They are ideal for centerpieces at weddings, showers, and graduation parties.

Time Required

1 to 2 hours

Supplies Needed

Adhesive shelf liner
Border punch
Etching cream
Paint pen

Step 1: Cut Shelf Liner
Use a border punch to cut a design from adhesive shelf liner. Adhere the design to the glass vase, smoothing out air bubbles.

Step 2: Spread the Etching Cream
Following the package instructions, spread a generous layer of etching cream onto the vase, covering the design. Leave the cream on for the instructed time, then rinse with water and remove the shelf liner.

Step 3: Paint Embellishments
If desired, finish the vase by adding accents using a paint pen.

opposite A clear-glass jar becomes a piece of art when painted with a simple flower-inspired design.

Time Required

1 to 2 hours

Supplies Needed

Willow twigs

Weather-resistant small nails

Birch bark (or other material such as tin flashing, copper, cedar shake, or scrap lumber)

Acrylic or latex paint

Polyurethane sealer or spray

Twig Plant Markers

Turn twigs and bits of wood or bark into distinctive plant markers. Willow is an excellent option for stick crafts.

Step 1: Cut and Nail Twigs
Cut four pieces of slender (¾ inch or so) willow or other twigs. Pieces should be long enough for a 3×5- or 4×4-inch plant marker. Nail together with copper nails or any weather-resistant small nails.

Step 2: Cut Birch Bark
Cut a piece of birch bark from a fallen tree to size. Or use whatever you have on hand—tin flashing, copper, a cedar shake, or scrap lumber. Nail to the back of the frame.

Step 3: Make Stake
To make a stake for the sign, nail a 16-inch or so branch to the back of the frame, extending the top of the stake above the sign as shown.

 TWISTED LOGIC

BHG TEST GARDEN TIP

Look for twigs with textured bark and interesting twists and turns to make attractive marker frames. You can also use twigs to create other stick-inspired crafts. Make a rustic picture frame by gluing twisted twigs onto a ready-made frame. Or create a twiggy table runner by weaving twigs together with jute cording.

Step 4: Paint the Plant Name
Use any acrylic or latex paint you have handy. Let dry, then coat entire label, including the ends of the stake, with a polyurethane sealer or spray.

Inspired by the bounty of the autumn
garden, this wreath can be hung
outdoors to feed the birds.

Harvest Wreath

The base of this fall wreath is the snipped-off top of a wire tomato cage, a fun way to put a garden discard to good use.

Time Required

1 hour

Supplies Needed

Tomato cage
Wire cutters
Jute
Pruners
Small ears of field corn
Gourds
Cranberries
Snowberries
Millet stalk
Pine boughs
Florist's wire
Ribbon

Step 1: Cut Off Top Layer
Snip off the top layer of a tomato cage, leaving the adjoining spokes attached to the wire circle.

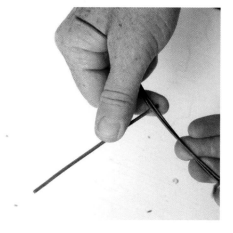

Step 2: Bend Wire Spokes
Bend back the spokes of the wire circle to make a flat-back wreath form.

Step 3: Wrap Wire
Wrap the wire circle with jute to give it a finished look. Slide small ears of corn and gourds onto the wire spokes, creating a balanced pattern.

Step 4: Add Berries
Top gourds with cranberries to hide the wires. Fill in the wire circle with snowberries as needed.

Step 5: Wire Additional Materials
Wire together millet, small pine boughs, and snowberries using florist's wire to make a finishing flourish. Tie the flourish to the wreath using ribbon.

Cracked-Pot Succulent Garden

Broken pots become more than they're cracked up to be when planted with hardy succulents.

Time Required

1 to 2 hours

Supplies Needed

Terra-cotta pot and shards (we used a 10-inch azalea pot)

Moistened cacti soil mix or a blend of equal parts lightweight soil mix and clean sand

Six or more assorted succulent plants

Bamboo skewers and garden shears or clippers

Clean pebbles and river rock

Soil scoop and small spoon

Richly textured succulents develop warm hues during cool fall weather. Clockwise, from top right: *Sedum sichotense*, mixed sempervivum varieties, and *Sedum lineare* 'Golden Teardrop'.

Step 1: Add Potting Mix
Begin by firmly pressing potting mix into the base of the pot, filling along the broken edge in front and building higher at the back.

Step 2: Plant Clumps
Gently separate clumps of plants and arrange them at the lowest point of the broken pot, overlapping the edge. Carefully press the roots onto the potting mix and backfill behind them. Add more plants and soil as desired, pressing soil firmly into place.

Step 3: Insert Shard
Place a large shard inside the pot, putting the broken edge at the base of the topmost plants to create a small retaining wall. Press the shard firmly into place, taking care not to cut the plant roots. Backfill with more potting mix, pressing it firmly into place.

Step 4: Continue Planting
Continue adding plants and broken pot pieces as desired. Carefully press root balls, shards, and soil into place, taking care to fill in edges and gaps to eliminate air pockets.

Step 5: Anchor Pot
When placing a small whole pot upright or at an interesting angle, anchor it by inserting a bamboo skewer through the drainage hole. Push the skewer down through the potting mix nearly to the bottom. If the skewer sticks out above the upright pot, cut it off with shears or clippers. Place a plant in the pot and press soil mix firmly around the edges of the root ball.

Step 6: Sprinkle Rocks
A few well-placed river rocks help hold shards, soil, and plants in place while adding a nice accent. A small spoon allows you to place pebbles on the soil around plants and tuck them in along edges. Finally, water thoroughly with a gentle stream; this helps settle everything into place. You should not need to water again for a week, then just a couple of times per week thereafter.

Time Required

1 to 2 hours

Supplies Needed

Flower petals
Pinecones
Autumn leaves
Berries
Cookie sheet
Scented oil
Orrisroot
Nonmetal container and
    utensil

Potpourri

Preserve the color and fragrance of your summer garden by drying blooms, buds, leaves, and seeds. Add essential-oil fragrance, then enjoy your garden's bounty all year. Place potpourri in bowls to scent a room or add it to small cloth bags and use as drawer fresheners.

Step 1: Dry Your Materials
Scatter flower petals, orange peels, pinecones, autumn leaves, and berries on a cookie sheet. Allow them to dry several days until either brittle or leathery.

Step 2: Add Essential Oils
Mix about 8 drops of your favorite essential oil (available at bath shops and health food stores) with 2 tablespoons orrisroot (available at pharmacies). Stir in a nonmetal container using a nonmetal utensil.

Step 3: Mix the Contents
Toss with 6 to 8 cups of the dried plant material. Place in an airtight container for several weeks. Then use.

BHG TEST GARDEN TIP

CITRUS SCENTS

Make a citrusy potpourri by combining the ingredients below. Pour the mixture into an airtight container and set aside to cure for three or four weeks.

- 3 tablespoons orrisroot
- ½ tablespoon lemon, lime, mandarin, or tangerine oil
- 1 cup dried orange rind
- ½ cup dried lemon rind
- 1 cup dried calendula flowers
- ¼ cup dried lemon thyme
- 1 cup dried lemon verbena
- ½ cup dried lemon balm
- 1 cup dried scented geranium leaves

GROW YOUR OWN POTPOURRI

Your garden's beds and borders can produce everything you need to make your own custom blends of potpourri. Here are some popular garden plants to grow for potpourri.

ROSES This romantic garden plant produces a variety of potpourri materials. Dried rosebuds make beautiful additions because they retain their flower form. Rose petals add color. And dried rose hips are beautiful and textural.

STRAWFLOWERS Popular for dried flower bouquets and potpourri, this flower produces petals that are dry and paperlike on the plant, so they don't require drying. Although strawflowers don't have scent, they offer beautiful flower color.

LAVENDER The fragrant flower buds, leaves, and stems of this plant offer a distinctive scent to potpourri. The buds retain their blue hue, so they look beautiful in any potpourri mix. Harvest flowers when they are just starting to open.

Idea 1

Idea 2

Idea 3

Dirt Tote

Idea 4

Salvaged Containers

Scour your attic for planting vessels that add interest and fun to your garden. Plus, these found-object containers are usually inexpensive or free.

Time Required

About 15 minutes

Supplies Needed

Potting soil

Plastic or terra-cotta containers of various sizes

Time-release pellet fertilizer

Salvaged display items, such as buckets, wheelbarrows, wagons, bicycles, tricycles, wire baskets, toy trucks, galvanized watering cans, and weathered wooden crates

Tired of terra-cotta? Take a shopping trip through your attic or garage and recruit unused or cast-off objects as creative garden displays. Rusty old bicycles, wheelbarrows, kids' wagons, even galvanized buckets make great-looking containers that will be the envy of the neighborhood.

Idea 1: Bench and Buckets

An old bench helps create layers of interest in this container grouping. Galvanized buckets and crusty terra-cotta pots filled with begonias cluster on ground level, while locker-room baskets discovered at a flea market draw the eye upward to showcase even more plants.

Idea 2: Tricked-Out Trike

Rejuvenate old objects into one-of-a-kind containers. Here, we transformed a beleaguered tricycle into a whimsical stage for prized plants. Potted petunias and white begonias create more visual impact when grouped than if they stood alone.

Idea 3: Creative Cart

A flower cart packed with elephant's ear, baby's tears, sweet potato vine, and petunias makes a lighthearted statement. Made from a hodgepodge of materials, the cart proves everything old can be new again. The bracket handles were constructed from old lamps, and the wheel is an antique.

Idea 4: Bicycle Still Life

Once used for toting lunch boxes and math books to school, the wire basket on this neglected bicycle finds new life as a display stand for plants. The weathered bike adds playful personality to the setting and serves as a fanciful focal point among the nearby flowers and shrubs.

ENSURE DRAINAGE

Before you add plants to any found-object container, make sure there is adequate drainage so plant roots don't sit in water. Drill several drainage holes in the base of a wheelbarrow, buckets, or other metal or wooden vessels. Sometimes the rusted treasures you find will already have their own weather-made drainage holes.

Painted Flowerpots

Add a cheerful face to plain terra-cotta flowerpots by dressing them in bold stripes. Choose a classic white stripe or improvise freehand with other colors and designs.

Time Required

1 to 2 hours

Supplies Needed

Terra-cotta pots
White enamel paint
Acrylic fixative
Narrow paintbrush
Masking tape (optional)

Step 1: Mark and Paint Stripes

Start with a clean, dry terra-cotta pot. Mark pencil points on the rim and bottom for spacing. Hand-paint stripes with white enamel, using the width of the paintbrush for spacing. Choose the brush according to the size of the pot. With hand-painting, it's OK if the stripes have slightly ragged edges. For a more controlled look, use masking tape to mark off the stripes.

Step 2: Paint the Rim

Paint the rim of the pot with white enamel. Allow the paint to dry thoroughly; brush on an acrylic fixative. For an interesting combination, paint the stripe motifs on pots of various sizes. Small ones are ideal for tabletop decorating and gifts. For added interest, you can paint the inside of the pot a solid color.

Magical Mosaics

Remnants of their former selves, broken pieces of tile, pottery, and glass find new purpose in garden mosaics.

Ever feel like you want to break something? Put that energy to good use by creating your own mosaic masterpieces. More than just a pretty face, mosaics can play a special role in your garden.

Creating mosaic art is like assembling a jigsaw puzzle, but without a picture to follow. You determine what patterns, colors, and shapes your artwork will take. Create crazy stepping-stones outfitted in a rainbow of colors or more subdued wall plaques from sophisticated porcelain china patterns. Lend sentimental value to your work by using an old dish set. Or turn an accident into a blessing by giving new life to a broken treasured memento.

Birdbaths, birdhouses, bowls, deck railings, containers, plant stands, watering cans, and chairs are all wonderful objects to dress in mosaic attire. So take a big swing. Smash an old dinnerware set, then reincarnate it as a wall plaque, serving tray, colorful pot, or stepping-stone. Every piece you create will be an original.

Time Required

1 to 2 hours

Supplies Needed

Surface to decorate, such as a
   pot or stepping-stone
Variety of tiles (plates, cups,
   glass, mirrors, marbles, and
   polished stones can be used in
   mosaics)
Dish towels
Hammer
Nippers
Protective goggles
Putty knife
Acrylic adhesive or thinset
   mortar
White grout (sanded or
   nonsanded)
Tinted grout (optional)
Soft rags and sponges
Rubber gloves
Silicone sealer
Foam paintbrush

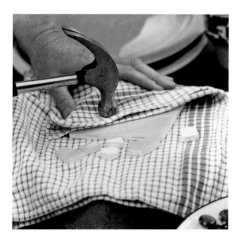

Step 1: Break It Up

Wrap the tile or pottery piece in towels on a hard surface, then pound with a hammer. Stop occasionally to check the size of the smashed pieces—you don't want them too small (not smaller than, say, a dime). As your pattern becomes more intricate, use nippers to further cut and shape the pieces into smaller sections. Always be sure to wear safety goggles when you use nippers to keep splinters out of your eyes.

Step 2: Use Your Imagination

Start arranging your pieces in the center of the terra-cotta container or stepping-stone and work your way out to the perimeter. Place the largest pieces first, then fill in with smaller pieces. Use a putty knife to butter each piece with acrylic adhesive or thinset, then position the pieces on the stone. Let the adhesive dry overnight.

Step 3: Fill In the Gaps

After 24 hours of drying time, prepare white grout or pretinted grout or create your own tinted grout. Mix the grout until it's the consistency of cake frosting. Wearing rubber gloves, smear the grout onto your design with a putty knife, pressing it into all the cracks and grooves as you work.

Step 4: Clean It Up

Wipe off excess grout with a wet rag or sponge, then give your design another wipe with a dry rag. Let the grout set for at least an hour, then buff it with a soft, dry rag. Let the piece cure for one week.

Step 5: Protect Your Work

Apply silicone sealer. Work in a well-ventilated area and apply the sealer with a foam paintbrush. Wipe the solution over the entire surface. Once it's absorbed, apply a second coat. Buff and polish the piece with a soft, dry rag.

BHG TEST GARDEN TIP

STEP LIGHTLY

Place your mosaic garden steppers into your garden, then plant thyme around the edges. This aromatic groundcover features tiny, fragrant leaves and flowers. Creeping varieties can handle moderate foot traffic. Tuck plants between the stepping-stones of a garden path. Plant thyme in full sun and well-drained soil. Zones 5–9.

Jar Luminarias

Cast a cool light on your deck or patio with these decorative candleholders. Pint-size canning jars, glazed with paint, make easy and pretty candle lanterns.

Time Required

6 to 8 hours

Supplies Needed

6 pint canning jars (or other clear glass container of your choice)

Floral spray paint

Plastic container of water

Eye protection

Dust mask

Tongs

Step 1: Select the Containers

Glass jars of any kind, vases, and deep bowls work well. Match candles to containers. Wide-mouth containers up to 6 inches tall can hold small pillar candles. Tea lights fit easily into half-pint glass jars and shallow bowls. You will also need a wide, shallow disposable container, such as a plastic pot saucer.

NOTE: Wear eye protection and a dust mask and do all your spraying outside on a calm day. Fill the plastic saucer with water. Use a floral-type spray paint, formulated for spraying colors on fresh or dried flowers; it's available from crafts stores and floral suppliers. Spray a light coat of paint on the water's surface.

Step 2: Dip and Rotate

Create the soft, mottled effect on the glass by dipping each container into the water and rotating it once to glaze with paint. To avoid fingerprints, use tongs. Coating the glass with too much paint diminishes the glazed effect. This method is not suitable for tableware used for serving or eating; the paint won't hold up to repeated washings.

Pansy Ball

Plant a ball filled with bloom. A pansy ball is an ideal project for the cool-weather days of spring and autumn, when these flowers do best.

Time Required

1 to 2 hours

Supplies Needed

Wire ball, 6–8 inches in diameter

Wire

Sphagnum moss

Potting soil

Flat of bedding plants, such as pansies, violas, ivy, or impatiens

If you're looking for something different to spruce up your outdoor surroundings, opt for these cheerful blooming spheres. We planted an heirloom favorite—pansies—in ours, but you can use a number of annuals to create yours. The cheerful balls of blossoms are perfect for hanging on a porch, near a door, or throughout the garden for eye-catching color. Their abundant blooms will last until a hard frost.

Step 1: Prepare the Sphere
Tuck sphagnum moss inside the ball, lining it from bottom to top, then fill the moss "nest" with potting soil. Carefully build up the sides, adding soil until the ball is filled. (If necessary, wrap additional wire around the ball so it will hold the moss in place.)

Step 2: Plant the Flowers
Poke holes into the moss and soil and insert pansies, violas, impatiens, or ivy, spacing plants about 2 inches apart. Press them far enough into the soil to assure they'll take hold quickly. Cover the entire sphere with plants. Water it well and place it in good light but not direct sunlight. For months of vivid color, keep the ball moist and deadhead the flowers frequently. If it becomes overgrown, cut it back to produce a new round of cheerful blossoms.

Tin-Can Luminarias

Brighten your deck or patio with these cheerful punched-tin lights. Even on a breezy summer evening, these inexpensive luminarias will set a festive mood. Constructed from discarded cans, they can be any size that works for a votive candle.

Time Required

1 to 2 hours

Supplies Needed

Empty, cleaned cans
Beer-can opener
Hammer
Nail or awl
Work gloves

Step 1: Clean Up Cans

Remove the labels, tops, and bottoms of the cans. (For our project, we used 26-ounce cans.) Wash thoroughly. Use an old-fashioned beer-can opener to make triangular holes around the perimeter of the top and bottom of each can. Wear work gloves and beware of sharp edges. Curl the flaps of metal loosely around the rims of the can.

Step 2: Make Holes

With a hammer and a sharp nail or awl, carefully punch additional holes in a pattern on the surface of each can. Aim for simple, stylized patterns. Work with a spare can or two for practice. If the can creases, insert a block of wood into the can to provide support while making the punch holes.

Step 3: Create a Base

Place each can in a terra-cotta saucer with a votive candle inside. For taller bases, glue a pair of saucers bottom to bottom. Vary the tall and short bases on your deck, patio, and tabletop for lively decorative interest.

opposite Tin-can luminarias are inexpensive options for big lighting events, such as lining the driveway for a holiday party. **left** Add festive can luminarias to an outdoor drink station.

Quick Verdigris

Take the glare off new garden ornaments by applying an aged-look finish. A new terra-cotta urn can sport a decades-old verdigris appearance in just an afternoon with a few simple steps, two colors of latex paint, and latex glazing liquid.

Time Required

1 to 2 hours

Supplies Needed

Terra-cotta pot
Black latex paint
Grayish green latex paint
Latex glazing liquid
Paintbrush
Clean cotton cloths
Flat clear sealer

Step 1: Clean and Paint Pot
Using a damp clean cloth, remove dirt and dust from the container. Allow to dry. Paint the container with the black latex paint. Allow it to dry.

Step 2: Make the Verdigris
Mix one part latex glazing liquid to four parts grayish-green latex paint. Paint the container with the verdigris.

Step 3: Blot and Dab
With a clean cotton cloth, blot and dab the verdigris glaze. If the glaze seems too thick or thin, adjust by adding more paint or glaze. Rub the glaze into crevices and dab off excess paint on the raised detailing to mimic the effects of aging.

Step 4: Add Sealer
Allow the pot to dry, then finish with three coats of flat clear sealer. Allow drying time between coats.

Paint-On Patina

If you want a garden accent to look as if it has been outside for decades, create instant patina. Simply speed up the aging process with caramel-color latex paint and latex glazing liquid.

> ## Time Required
> 1 to 2 hours
>
> ## Supplies Needed
> New concrete garden sculpture
> Base coat: off-white paint
> Top coat: caramel-color paint
> Latex glazing liquid
> Paintbrush
> Clean cloths
> Sealer

Step 1: Make the Patina Paint
Mix three to four parts caramel-color paint to one part latex glazing liquid. Adjust with paint or glaze as needed to achieve a pleasing color.

Step 2: Add the Base Coat
Brush on a coat of off-white paint with a paintbrush. Use a cloth to rub the paint into the folds and crevices.

Step 3: Add the Patina
Rub on the patina mixture with a clean cloth. Allow to dry. Dab on patches of diluted off-white base paint. Blend by rubbing gently with a clean cloth.

Step 4: Seal It
After the base coat dries, spray on a light coat of sealer to protect the finish. If the basecoat fails to cover adequately, apply a second coat.

above An adorable garden nymph looks like an antiquity (instead of a new statue) with painted patina.

Leaf-Embossed Flowerpots

Plain terra-cotta flowerpots are attractive and useful, but rarely the stars of the garden. Transform these ordinary flowerpots into works of art. This easy painting project uses real leaves as patterns to create graphic elements inspired by nature.

Time Required

1 to 2 hours

Supplies Needed

Leaves
Exterior latex paint
Portland cement
Concrete bonding adhesive
Dust mask
Paintbrush
Sponge
Clean cloth

right Foliage plants such as bird's-nest fern, *left,* and begonia, *right,* look stunning in leaf-pattern containers.

Step 1: Mix Paint
While mixing and applying this paint mixture, wear rubber gloves and a dust mask. Pour one part water into a mixing container and shake in two parts portland cement. Add one part concrete bonding adhesive. Mix to the consistency of heavy whipping cream. Brush the mixture onto the ribbed side of the leaf.

Step 2: Press Leaf
Press the leaf to the dry pot with your fingers, then with a damp sponge. Wipe away mix that seeps out. Leave on for 1 to 2 minutes.

Step 3: Peel Off Leaf
Carefully peel away the leaf. Reuse the leaf or decorate your pot with leaves in different sizes and shapes. Allow the pot to dry for 5 minutes.

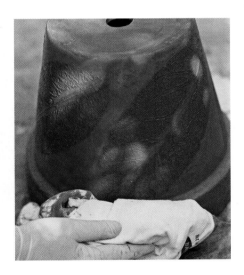

Step 4: Make and Apply Wash
Mix a color wash of 4 ounces water, 4 ounces exterior latex paint, and 2 tablespoons bonding adhesive. Paint the pot and wait a minute. Apply the wash. Wipe in a circular motion with a cloth. The concrete areas will appear burnished.

BHG TEST GARDEN TIP

CHOOSING LEAVES

Chose one or more fresh, thick, supple leaves to use as your stamps for this project. The ideal leaves will have pronounced raised veins on the underside.

For a different look, hold the clean side of the leaf against the pot and brush around the edges with the paint mixture. Try this silhouetting technique around the rim of the pot. If you aren't happy with the results, wipe off and try again. Or touch up problem spots with a small artist's brush.

Pussy Willow Wreath

Among the first hopeful signs of spring are the sweet fuzzy buds of common varieties of pussy willow. While snipping pussy willow branches and bringing them indoors is a treat, why not go a step further and turn them into a long-lasting wreath?

Time Required

1 to 2 hours

Supplies Needed

48 pussy willow branches, each approximately 4 feet long

Wire cutters

Paper-covered 26-gauge florist's wire

6-inch-diameter grapevine wreath base

BHG TEST GARDEN TIP — GROWING PUSSY WILLOWS

Pussy willows are great garden plants. They offer privacy and provide that first touch of spring. Pussy willows prefer full sun and moist soil. They don't mind wet feet, so they can be grown in rain gardens.

Pussy willows are fast-growing plants that benefit from pruning each spring. Trimming shapes the plant, keeps its growth in check, and encourages prolific blooms. Pussy willows grow vigorously; if you cut one down to a 6-inch stump, it will grow back in two to three years. Young shrubs can grow as much as 6 feet per year; left unpruned, they become overgrown and beyond easy reach. Mature plants grow 2–4 feet per year but continue to benefit from annual pruning.

Step 1: Cut the Willows
On a work surface, cut pussy willow branches into 8- to 10-inch lengths. Save extra branch pieces for filling in openings that will appear once the branches have dried.

Step 2: Make a Bundle
Gather six to eight branch pieces in one hand and form a fan-shape bundle.

Step 3: Attach to Frame
Secure the bundle using a 5-inch length of paper-covered wire. Attach the bundle to the wreath base, twisting the wire ends to hold the branch pieces in place. Repeat until the wreath base is covered.

...lent-packed frames make ...iful vertical mini gardens. ...lents are easy-care plants ...equire minimal watering.

Framed Succulent Garden

Create a living masterpiece using soil as the canvas, plants as paint, and a picture frame as a planter. Then hang up your living succulent art for everyone to admire.

A succulent "painting" will last for years with little upkeep because these plantings are so easy-care. You can keep the price of your vertical planter to a minimum by using an inexpensive flea market picture frame. If you have succulents in your garden, use cuttings for your project.

Choose succulent varieties that stay small. Hens-and-chicks, echeveria, and sedums are ideal because they won't overgrow the small space.

Limit your palette to three or four colors and select different varieties of succulents within that color scheme.

Create a river of color through the picture. Form a diagonal swath of one color, either with one type of plant or with different varieties in the same color scheme. Give your picture a focal point with a cluster of succulents or one large specimen such as *Aeonium*. Although the plant will eventually outgrow your picture, you can pull it out when it overgrows the others and replace it with something else.

Time Required

1 to 2 hours

Supplies Needed

Succulent cuttings

Picture frame with back and glass removed

Shadow box made of redwood or cedar 1×3s cut to fit the back of the frame

Hammer or screwdriver

Nails or screws

½-inch hardware cloth, cut to fit the inside dimensions of the frame

Staple gun and staples

¼-inch plywood backing, cut to fit the back of the shadow box

Exterior paint

Clean cloth (optional)

All-purpose potting mix

Chopstick or pencil

Step 1: Take Cuttings
With small pruning snips, cut stem sections 1–2 inches long from established succulent plants. Remove lower leaves (roots will sprout from these leaf nodes). Let cuttings dry on a tray for a few days before planting them; this curing process causes cut ends to callus, or form a thin layer of cells. It's OK if the cuttings shrivel up a little bit.

Step 2: Add a Shadow Box
Nail or screw the shadow box in place. The naturally water-resistant redwood or cedar box will add depth and allow space for soil and plants.

Step 3: Set Hardware Cloth
With the frame still facedown, insert hardware cloth. Staple hardware cloth to the edges of the frame. The ½-inch grid is small enough to hold in potting soil yet large enough to accommodate stems.

Step 4: Attach Backing
Lay ¼-inch plywood backing onto the back of the shadow box. Secure with nails.

Step 5: Paint the Frame
Turn the frame face up. Brush on a coat of exterior paint to offer some protection against the elements. For an antique effect, let the paint dry for a few minutes and then wipe the frame with a clean cloth. If desired, paint the underlying box, too. Let dry completely before filling the box with potting mix.

Step 6: Add Soil
Pour soil on top of the hardware cloth, using your hands to push it through the openings. Shake the frame periodically to evenly disperse the soil. Add more soil until it reaches the bottom of the wire grid.

Step 7: Create a Design
On a flat surface, lay out succulent cuttings in the design you want in the frame. Push a chopstick or pencil through one square of the wire grid and into the soil.

Step 8: Begin Planting
Place the stem of a succulent cutting, such as this mother of pearl plant (*Graptopetalum paraguayense*), into the planting hole, allowing the leaf rosette to rest atop the wire grid. It's not necessary to dip cuttings in rooting hormone—succulents root easily in soil.

Step 9: Continue Planting
Tuck in larger plants first, followed by smaller ones, planting as close together as the grid allows. Depending on plant size, not every square will be planted. After planting, you might see hints of the wire, but as the succulents grow, they'll close the gaps.

Step 10: Let It Root
After planting, keep the living succulent picture flat and out of direct sunlight for a week or two to allow cuttings to form roots along the stems. (For additional security, support stems with florist's pins or crafts clips.)

Step 11: Increase Light
Gradually increase light levels to full-sun exposure. Do not water during the first two weeks.

Step 12: Display Your Picture
Set the living succulent picture on a table or shelf near a south-facing window where it can be propped against a wall. Or hang the frame on a wall with sturdy picture hooks. Water succulents once a month by laying the frame on a flat surface and thoroughly moistening the soil; make sure the frame is dry before you rehang it. In hot areas, protect plants from midday sun.

Porch Shades

Ambitious alfresco fabrics turn simple projects into grand decorating schemes as great as all outdoors. Equipped with an easy-to-install pulley system, these porch draperies are crafted from 60-inch-wide screening found at hardware stores. If you can find only narrower widths, stitch them together to create right-size panels for your porch.

Time Required
2 to 4 hours
Supplies Needed
60-inch-wide screening
Aquamarine outdoor fabric
Sewing machine
Nickel-plated grommets and hooks
Pulleys
Nylon line
Chrome-plated cleats

Step 1: Fashion the Panels
We cut the screening to the desired length and then framed each panel with aquamarine outdoor fabric. We folded 10-inch-wide strips in half to form 5-inch-wide borders, turned the raw edges under, mitered the corners, and pinned the strips in place so they encased the edges of the screening. Then we topstitched through the fabric and screening.

Step 2: Add the Grommets
Grommets in the top corners of the panels allow them to hang from hooks on the porch overhang. Pulleys on the outer hooks raise and lower the panels. A grommet placed one-third of the way down on the inside of each panel accommodates the nylon line that runs from the top outside corner through the pulley, making a tieback.

Step 3: Raise the Curtains
To let the sunshine in, raise the panels and tie the nylon line to the chrome-plated cleats bolted onto the bottom of the porch columns. Marine supply and hardware stores stock pulleys, cleats, and nylon line that will endure the elements.

Curtains dress up a front porch, making it feel special as well as enclosed for privacy purposes.

Twisted Topiary

Layer spirals of ivy and moss to make a conifer-shape decoration that glows with greenery. This treelike topiary can be any size you want, as long as you scale it to the pot size. (The example pictured is about 18 inches tall, and the pot is 8 inches square.) Plan to use plants and mosses of contrasting textures and colors so the individual spirals are distinct.

Time Required

1 to 2 hours

Supplies Needed

Chicken wire

Wire cutter

Decorative pot

Potting mixture

Sphagnum moss

Floral pins

Green or silver reindeer moss

Plants

right Ivy is the ideal vining plant for topiaries. Varieties come in different leaf hues, including deep green, blue-green, frosted white, and variegated.

Step 1: Craft and Fit the Cone
Cut the chicken wire and bend it into a cone shape. Fold over any protruding wires. Place about 2 inches of sterilized potting mix into the pot. Make sure the cone fits in the pot; adjust if needed.

Step 2: Make It Mossy
Remove the cone, turn it over, and fill it with wet sphagnum moss. Pack the moss firmly enough so it won't sag when the cone is upright, but avoid packing it so tightly you can't insert plants.

Step 3: Secure the Cone
Place the filled cone inside the pot and use floral pins to secure the base in the potting mixture. About six pins should suffice.

Step 4: Make a Sphagnum Spiral
Starting at the top, use green moss or silver reindeer moss to create a spiral all the way down the tree. Leave a gap of 2–3 inches between the runs of the spiral. Secure the moss to the sphagnum base with floral pins.

Step 5: Insert the Plants
Poke a finger through the chicken wire into the sphagnum moss to make depressions for the plants. Leave a bit of soil clinging to the roots and carefully bed the plants in the sphagnum moss.

Step 6: Pin the Plants
Secure the plants and any long stems that stick out to the sphagnum base using additional floral pins. Continue to fill in bare spots until the cone is covered. Stand back and admire your handiwork.

Time Required

1 to 2 days

Supplies Needed

Plywood

Saw

Hammer

1½-inch finishing nails

Sakrete sand mix (available from
    home improvement stores)

Bucket or other large container

Trowel

Cardboard box

Staddle Stones

Originally employed as architectural supports, traditional staddle stones make delightful decorative garden elements.

Standing like large toadstools, staddle stones were used for centuries to elevate barn floors off the ground, helping to keep grain dry and free of rodents. Now you can make your own miniature versions for garden ornaments, using sand mix and an easy-to-build mold. The stones consist of a base and mushroomlike cap. Our version stands approximately 12 inches high, but you can make yours any size you desire by adjusting the form. Create miniature versions to decorate tabletops or set in a flowerbed, along a garden path, in an alpine trough, or on a mantel. Group them beside a pond or water garden or place them in miniature conservatories.

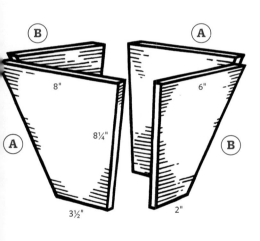

Step 1: Form the Base
To make the form for the base, cut four pieces of plywood to the sizes shown, making two A pieces and two B pieces. Fit the pieces together with finishing nails so that the A pieces are opposite each other. Don't nail the form tightly; you'll need to spread apart the sides to pop out the base once it sets.

Step 2: Pack It with Sand
Prepare the sand mix in a bucket or other large container according to package instructions. A 20-pound bag of Sakrete mix will make about eight 12-inch-high stones. For the base, pack the plywood form with sand mix, filling it as full as you want the height of the base. Level the top of the mix by tapping the side of the form with the trowel. Let it sit overnight. When it is dry, pry the form apart slightly and pop out the base.

Step 3: Cap It Off
Place a layer of sand at least 5 inches deep in a cardboard box. Dampen the sand. Using a mixing bowl, make a depression that matches the desired size of the cap. Fill the depression with sand mix. Tamp it down. Let it sit overnight. Remove the cap from the box. Let both the base and the cap dry for a day. Set the cap on top of the base.

Once your gourds are dried and painted, they will last for years.

Gourd Luminarias

Gourds make pretty autumn decorations when dried, painted, and stained.
Turn them into luminarias to enhance a holiday mood.

How to Dry Gourds

Step 1: Buy or Grow Gourds
Pick gourds that are firm and free of blemishes before drying them. Always purchase or grow extra gourds; it's common for 25 percent or more of the gourds to mold during drying.

Step 2: Dry Gourds
Place freshly picked ones in a warm, dry place that has good air circulation.

Step 3: Turn Gourds
Check and turn the gourds every week. Drying may take anywhere from a few weeks to several months, depending on the size and moisture content of the gourd and the humidity and warmth of your drying area.

Step 4: Remove Skins
Once the gourds are dry, they will have a paperlike skin that needs to be removed. Soak the gourds in warm water and keep them damp while working at this stage. Using a paring knife or crafts knife, gently scrape the skin from the gourd.

Step 5: Allow to Fully Dry
Let the gourd dry thoroughly before painting, drawing, or cutting.

How to Make Luminarias

Step 1: Draw Cutting Line
To make cutting the gourds easier and help prevent cracking and breaking, draw the cutting line with a pencil.

Step 2: Cut Gourds
Using a crafts knife, puncture small slits along the pencil line so it resembles a dotted line. Use the knife to cut between the lines. Smooth out any uneven spots. Using the crafts knife, cut a 3-inch round hole in the bottom of each gourd.

Step 3: Remove the Seeds
Clean out the inside material.

Step 4: Burn the Design
Working in a well-ventilated room or outdoors, use the woodburning tool to burn a circle through the gourd. Burn two more holes to create the three-dot triangular motif. Repeat the burning process around the entire gourd.

Step 5: Paint the Gourd
Use a light coat of raw umber watercolor. Use the brown marker to make stripes on the stems. After the paint dries, spray the gourds with varnish.

Step 6: Add a Tea Light
Place a tea light in a votive cup and slip the gourd over the cup. Make sure the candle's wick is trimmed short so the flame does not touch the gourd.

Time Required

7 to 8 hours

Supplies Needed

Dried gourds with stems
   attached
Crafts knife
Straight-sided votive cups
Woodburning tool with a
   ¼-inch-diameter round tip
Raw umber watercolor
Paintbrush
Brown marker
Water-base spray varnish
Tea-light candles

GROW YOUR OWN GOURDS
Bottle gourds are also called birdhouse gourds because their dried fruits can be made into birdhouses. Plant seeds in early spring. They need to grow 150–180 days before they are mature. Harvest ornamental gourds when the vines begin to dry and the shell has hardened. Leave 1–2 inches of the stem attached.

Window Box

Shimmering copper embossed with a stencil snowflake warms up a window box for the holidays. Snowflake string lights offer twinkly ambience after the sun sets.

Time Required

1 to 2 hours

Supplies Needed

Window box

Copper sheeting

Copper nails

C-5 light fixture with electrical cord and clear bulb

Staples

Sand or soil

Preserved or real evergreen shrubs of various sizes

Foam sheets or blocks (optional)

Copper-color spray paint

Glue sticks

Small wooden stars or other ornaments

Sheet moss

Step 1: Take Measurements

Measure the front panel and two side panels of your window box. Add 2 inches to the length of each side panel to allow room for the light fixture. Add another 1–2 inches to the top and bottom of each panel measurement for end caps, which will be folded over and nailed into the window box to eliminate sharp edges. Ask a metal fabricator to make three copper sheeting panels (one for the front and one for each side) to fit your measurements.

Step 2: Make the Snowflake

Use a photocopier to enlarge a snowflake pattern onto white paper to desired size. Measure and mark with pencil on the pattern where punch holes should be loaded. With masking tape, attach the pattern to the front copper panel, then punch holes at each mark using the metal punch and mallet. Punch nail holes into the corners of end caps, fold the tops and bottoms of the two side panels over the window box, and nail through the punched holes to secure.

Step 3: Add Lights and Paint

Place the light fixture so that it will be visible behind the punched design of the front cover; run the cord under the box to an electrical outlet. Staple around the cord to hold it in place. Leaving 2 inches of space between the window box and the front copper panel, fold the end caps over the box, and nail through the punched holes to secure. Spray-paint the wooden ornaments with copper-color paint; let dry. Hot-glue the ornaments to the preserved evergreen shrubs as decorations. If using real evergreens, simply attach. Arrange the evergreen shrubs into a line, then mound sheet moss around evergreen shrubs as a festive edging.

Tile Bed Edgers

Dress up the borders of your flowerbeds with these handmade edging tiles made from terra-cotta floor tiles and cut with a jigsaw.

Time Required

1 to 4 hours

Supplies Needed

Terra-cotta floor tiles
Cardboard
Pencil
Jigsaw
Foundation sealer

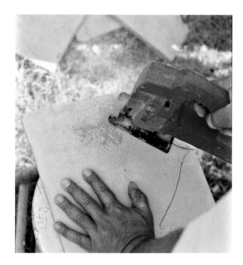

A decoratively edged border adds artistic flair to your garden all year round. These edgers are so easy to make, and your own design gives you a custom look.

Measure your garden bed and calculate how many tiles you'll need. To make our calculations easier, we chose ½-inch-thick, 12-inch-square terra-cotta floor tiles. Using a tile-size sheet of thin cardboard, sketch your design. To make cutting easier, stick to simple shapes and gentle curves. Also allow at least 4 inches of tile to be sunk into the ground. Cut out your design template and use a pencil to trace the shape onto your tiles.

Step 1: Draw and Cut the Design
Use a jigsaw blade designed for cutting tile to trim tiles into shape. (Always wear eye protection and a dust mask when cutting tile.) If trimming tiles is beyond your comfort level, hire out the job. For best results, buy or rent a heavy-duty jigsaw.

Step 2: Seal and Insert the Edgers
Dip the lower 4 inches of cut tiles into a bucket of foundation sealer to prevent the porous edges from crumbling. Let tiles dry overnight. Use a mattock, square-pointed shovel, or trowel to excavate a trench for the tiles. Dig the trench 4 inches deep and 1 inch wide. Remove sod, roots, and rocks. Stand tiles side by side in the trench. Backfill to hold them securely in place.

Birdbath in a Flash

You don't need an expensive and ornate birdbath to make a dramatic statement in the garden (or to entice birds!). This budget-friendly birdbath is easy to make with terra-cotta pots and a saucer. The result is a fanciful focal point for any corner of the garden.

Time Required

About 15 minutes

Supplies Needed

Two different sizes of terra-cotta pots (a 12-inch pot and 16-inch pot work well)
Large terra-cotta saucer

Step 1: Site Your Birdbath
Birds prefer an open area in which to bathe and drink, with shrubs or trees as a backdrop in the event they need to make a quick getaway.

Step 2: Stack the Pots
Place the smaller terra-cotta pot on top of the larger pot so that they fit snugly. Make sure the pots are solidly seated on the ground.

Step 3: Set the Saucer
Set a large saucer atop the containers. Ensure that the saucer is not so large that it tips easily.

Step 4: Fill the Basin
Add fresh, clean water.

right Entice colorful birds to your garden by keeping water in the dish all summer.

Bird Buffet

A perfect project for a bird-loving woodworker, this gorgeous Mission-style bird feeder will lure colorful songbirds to your yard all year long. Its solid construction and furniture-quality good looks will make it a yard ornament for years to come.

Time Required

About 7 hours

Supplies Needed

Table saw

Mortising machine (optional)

Drill

Chisel

Sander

Clamps

½×5½×6-inch hardware cloths (2)

¹⁄₁₆-inch aircraft cable,
    24 inches long

¹⁄₁₆-inch cable ferrules (3)

No. 8×1½-inch flathead
    wood screws (4)

No. 9 double-point staples (2)

Tin snips

Glue

Wood parts (see chart, page 104)

Clear exterior oil finish

Suet cake

right Seed-eating birds, such as chickadees and cardinals, will visit your feeder several times a day to stock up.

Bird Buffet

WOOD PARTS CUT TO SIZE
(All dimensions in inches)

	A	B	C	D
Thickness	¾	¾	¾	⅜
Width	3	3	2¾	⅜
Length	10	8	6⅛	¼
Material	C	C	C	W
Quantity	1	2	1	4

MATERIALS KEY:

C=choice (mahogany, redwood, cedar, teak, or cypress)

W=walnut or other dark hardwood

Step 1: Start with the Top

Cut the top (A) to size. We used mahogany, but redwood, cedar, teak, or cypress would work.

Raise your table-saw blade 1½ inches above the surface of the saw table. Angle the blade 25 degrees from vertical and away from the rip fence. Position the fence ¼ inch away from the bottom edge of the blade.

Using a push block or fence saddle to keep your fingers safely away from the blade, bevel-rip both ends of the top (A) and the edges. Cut the two sides (B) to 3×8 inches. To house the ½-inch hardware cloth (galvanized wire mesh), cut a pair of ⅛-inch grooves ¼ inch deep on the inside face of each, where shown on Side View, *opposite*.

Mark the location and cut a ¾-inch dado ¼ inch deep in each side (B) where dimensioned.

Locate and cut a pair of ⅜-inch-square mortises ⅛ inch deep on the outside face of each side (B), centering the mortises over the dado. (We cut ours with a mortising machine; you could also form them by drilling a hole and squaring the sides with a chisel.) Now drill a 5/32-inch shank hole, centered in each mortise.

Mark the angled cuts along both edges and the curved cut on the bottom ends of the sides (B). Cut and sand to the marked lines to complete each side piece.

Step 2: Add the Bottom

Cut the bottom (C) to size, bevel-ripping the edges at 4 degrees. You want the beveled edges of the bottom to be flush with the angled outside edges of the sides (B).

Cut two ⅛-inch grooves ¼ inch deep on the top face of the bottom (C) to align with the grooves in the sides (B).

Clamp (but do not glue) the bottom (C) between the sides (B). Check for square. Center the top (A) on the assembly and mark the hole locations for the cable on the bottom side of the top. The holes should be flush with the inside face of each side piece. Remove the top and drill the 3/16-inch holes where marked.

With the sides (B) and bottom (C) still dry-clamped together, use a tin snips to cut two pieces of hardware cloth to fit snugly into the ⅛-inch grooves. Next, using the shank holes in the mortises as guides, drill pilot holes 1½ inches deep into the ends of the bottom.

Remove the clamp and disassemble the bottom and sides (B, C). Sand all four pieces.

SIDE VIEW

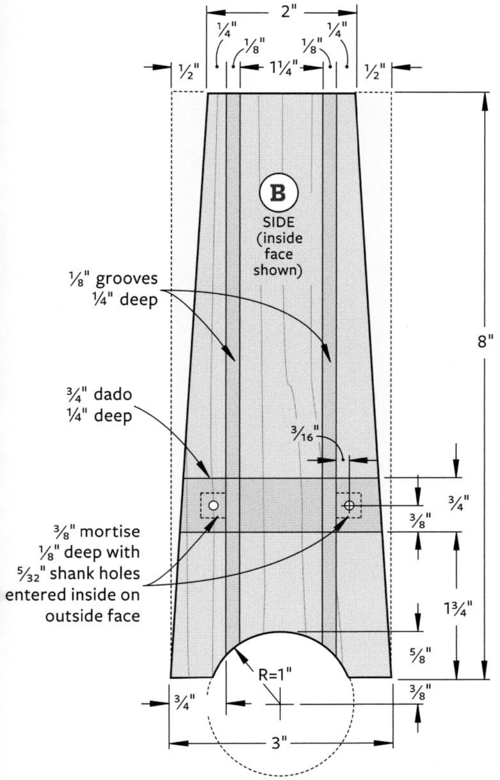

2"
1/4"
1/4"
1/8"
1/8"
1/2"
1 1/4"
1/2"
B
SIDE (inside face shown)
1/8" grooves 1/4" deep
8"
3/4" dado 1/4" deep
3/16"
3/4"
3/8"
3/8" mortise 1/8" deep with 5/32" shank holes entered inside on outside face
1 3/4"
5/8"
R=1"
3/8"
3/4"
3"

EXPLODED VIEW

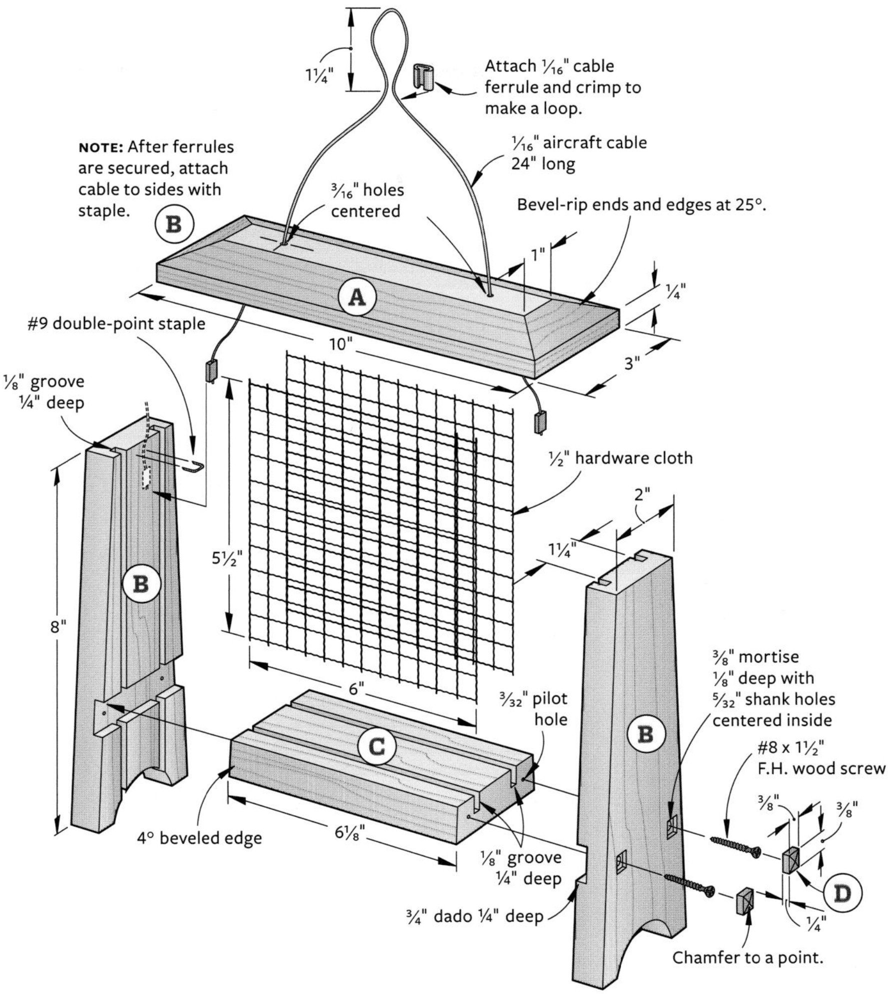

1 1/4"
Attach 1/16" cable ferrule and crimp to make a loop.
1/16" aircraft cable 24" long
NOTE: After ferrules are secured, attach cable to sides with staple.
3/16" holes centered
Bevel-rip ends and edges at 25°.
B
1"
A
1/4"
#9 double-point staple
10"
3"
1/8" groove 1/4" deep
1/2" hardware cloth
2"
1 1/4"
5 1/2"
B
8"
6"
3/32" pilot hole
C
3/8" mortise 1/8" deep with 5/32" shank holes centered inside
B
#8 x 1 1/2" F.H. wood screw
3/8"
3/8"
4° beveled edge
6 1/8"
1/8" groove 1/4" deep
D
3/4" dado 1/4" deep
1/4"
Chamfer to a point.

Step 3: Time for Assembly

Cut a piece of 1/16-inch aircraft cable to 24 inches long. Loop the top center section, where shown on Exploded View, *above right*, and crimp a cable ferrule 1 1/4 inches from the top end of the loop. Slide the ends of the cable through the holes in the top (A). Then crimp a ferrule onto each end of the cable where shown on the drawing.

Staple just above the ferrules on the ends of the cable to secure the cable to the inside face of each side (B), as shown in the photo on *page 103*.

Cut a 10-inch length of 3/8-inch-square dark stock. (We used walnut. You could also use mahogany and a black permanent marker to stain the stock.) Sand chamfers to form a point on both ends. (We did this on a disc sander.) Next, crosscut a 1/4-inch-long plug (D) from each end of the stock. Repeat the process to form another set of plugs.

Fit the bottom (C) between the sides. Drive the screws through the previously drilled shank and pilot holes. Check for square. Glue one plug in each mortise to hide the screw head. Apply a clear exterior penetrating oil finish. Slide the two pieces of hardware cloth in place, insert a cake of suet, and hang in an inviting location.

CHAPTER THREE

Water Wonders

Enjoy the musical sounds of moving water in your yard or patio. Take the dive into water gardening.

Tabletop Water Garden

Grab a shallow container, buy a few water-garden plants, and turn on the tap. You can have a pretty, miniature water garden in just minutes.

Time Required

1 to 2 hours

Supplies Needed

Container that can hold water

Water plants, such as water lettuce, azolla, water hyacinth, duckweed, and frog bit

Tap water

Liquid fertilizer

Step 1: Source a Container
The container should be watertight. A shallow container works well. You can buy a container for this water garden, or you can rummage around the kitchen for a shallow bowl, copper pot, or glass dish.

Step 2: Select Water Plants
Most garden centers and aquarium stores carry a variety of water plants. The best options for a small tabletop water garden such as this are "floater"-type plants. These simply float on the water surface; in a clear glass container, their roots will also add interest.

Step 3: Add Water and Plants
Fill the container with water and drop in the plants. Arrange them like you would a bouquet—mix up the textures.

opposite Easy and low-care, a tabletop dish filled with floating water plants gives you the reflective quality of water without the work of a full-scale water garden.

BHG TEST GARDEN TIP

WATER-GARDEN CARE
Check water levels daily. Change the water whenever it becomes murky or starts to give off any odor, which usually means once or twice a week. Fertilize very lightly with a liquid fertilizer each time you change the water.

Bell Fountain

Add the sound of water to your patio with this easy-to-install in-ground fountain. It's an ideal garden focal point.

An underground reservoir captures the water and houses the pump and components that make this pretty fountain function. A safe water feature for homes with small children, the fountain and its covered reservoir reduce safety concerns while still offering the joy of moving water in the landscape.

Personalize your fountain by using any fountainhead you like. A bell-shape fountainhead is used here, but the step-by-step process is the same for any fountainhead you choose. Create more splash and drama with a geyser or multitier sprayhead. If you would like to turn an urn or other decorative object into a fountain, simply run the vinyl tubing through the vessel rather than attaching a fountainhead.

Time Required

1 to 2 hours

Supplies Needed

Shovel
Preformed pond liner
Tarp or wheelbarrow
Sand
Pump
Rigid PVC pipe long enough to extend from the fountain to the nearest electrical outlet
Fountainhead, bell-shape
Window screening
Concrete block and rocks
Heavy-duty resin grate
Jigsaw
Zip ties
Hose clamp
River rock

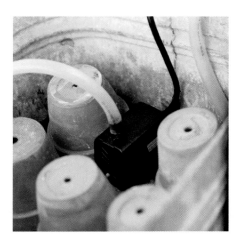

Step 1: Place the Pump
Place the pump, with tubing attached, in the bottom of the tub, making sure the intake faces downward. Fill the bottom of the tub with upside-down clay pots (or other filler).

Step 2: Layer Rocks
Layer rocks over the pots, but don't pile them up to the tub's rim yet. Make sure the tubing is positioned where you plan to set the bucket. For example, if you intend to place the bucket in one corner of the tub, be sure that's where you place the tubing so that you can easily run it up through the bucket. Run the pump's power cord up and out of the tub.

Step 3: Drill a Hole
Drill a hole in the bottom of the bucket, near the edge. The necessary hole size depends on the particular pump and tubing you use, but it should be no larger than the minimum that will accept the tubing. This could require a fairly large drill bit, perhaps ¾ inch or more. If you don't have a bit that size, you can drill several smaller holes in a tight cluster, then use a hammer to drive a chisel through. File away any sharp points.

Step 4: Add Tubing
Run the tubing up through the hole in the bottom of the bucket. The end should extend at least several inches above the bucket's top rim. Place the bucket in its final position within the rock-filled tub. To tilt the bucket so the water spills to one side, place a rock under the bucket to give the desired tilt.

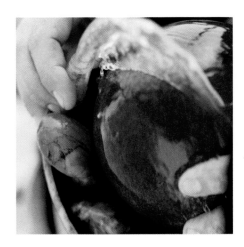

Step 5: Fill the Tub
Fill the remainder of the tub and the bucket with rocks; keep the tubing in place. Set the gazing ball on top of the rocks in the bucket, running the tubing up its back side (opposite the side from which the fountain will be viewed). Fill the tub, then plug in the pump. Adjust tubing so the water creates the desired pattern. Use rocks to hold it in place.

BHG TEST GARDEN TIP

FOUNTAIN FACTORS

One nice thing about this fountain is that even after it's completed, you can adjust the position of the bucket, rocks, and tubing to change the appearance and pattern of the fountain. This fountain loses water quickly through evaporation and splashing; check the water level before each use. Rinse the rocks and other materials with water before assembling the fountain so you start with clear water. Periodically drain and refill the fountain to keep the water fresh.

Pond in a Box

This miniature ecosystem brings the pleasure of a water garden to your deck or patio.

If you don't have the space for an in-ground water garden, don't despair. You can still enjoy your own aquatic haven by crafting this pond-in-a-box project that easily fits on an apartment balcony or a deck or patio. As long as you can pound a nail and use a screwdriver, you can do this. Add some water and a variety of small plants, and you'll have a small-scale pond to relish up close and personal throughout the growing season.

Time Required

2 to 4 hours

Supplies Needed

Wood

Handsaw or circular saw

Hammer and nails

Drill

Wood screws and screwdriver

Water sealant

Plastic liner

Water plants (we used Japanese sweet flag, arrowhead, common duckweed, stonecrop, houseleek, deer fern, and blue-eyed grass)

Potting soil

Pea gravel

Gazing ball or other ornament

opposite A deckside water garden is fun for the whole family. Add goldfish or small koi to consume mosquito larvae.

Step 1: Gather the Materials

We used 1×8 cedar boards for this project. (You can also use 1×10 or 1×12 boards to create a deeper pond.) Cut 30-inch lengths for the sides and 15-inch lengths for the ends. After assembling the outer frame, measure the interior dimension for the base of the box. Use the same 1×8 material for the base or use ¾-inch exterior plywood. Make sure you get straight cuts to minimize gapping.

Pond in a Box

Step 2: Build the Box
Predrill holes every 6 inches along the edges of the sides and ends to attach to the bottom piece. Use wood screws to connect the boards, attaching one long side to the base first, then following with the two short sides and finishing with the remaining long side. If you want to create a divider—a separate planting bed within the box—cut another piece of wood. Before attaching the divider, try it in different locations within your box until you get a look you like. The divider will isolate the water feature from the planting space. We divided our container so one-third is for plants and two-thirds is for the water garden.

Step 3: Secure the Ends
Use additional wood screws to fasten the end joints together, drawing the screws tight to minimize gapping. Apply sealant to lengths of 1×2-inch strips of wood and fasten them to the end joints; they will add strength to the box, dress it up, and provide additional sealing.

Step 4: Prepare the Inside
On the inside of the box, install a plastic liner (available at your local nursery) or use a water sealant safe for aquatic life (if you plan to add fish). Read the directions on the sealant can for the suggested number of coats, then do one more. Coat both the water area and the garden section. On the garden side, drill two or three holes in the floor to provide drainage for plants.

WATER PLANTS

Aquatic plants come in many shapes and textures. Combine several to create a healthier water garden that looks great, too.

WATER LILIES These showy plants have leaves that float on the water surface and beautiful blooms that look almost waxy. For a small pond, consider a hardy pygmy variety, such as *Nymphaea pygmaea* 'Alba' (white) or *Nymphaea tetragona* 'Helvola' (yellow); each covers less than 3 square feet of water surface.

OXYGENATING GRASSES Sometimes referred to as "water weed," these lacy-leaf plants add oxygen to the water. Consider planting anacharis (*Elodea canadensis*), which grows graceful, fernlike fronds in water 6 inches to 5 feet deep. Or plant water milfoil (*Myriophyllum*), which grows in water 6–30 inches deep and has green or reddish foliage.

FLOATING PLANTS These plants float on top, trailing roots below. The roots provide excellent cover for water creatures. To plant, simply plop them into the pond. Consider water hyacinth (*Eichhornia crassipes*) or water lettuce (*Pistia stratiotes*). Both plants are prolific growers, so thin them by hand if they spread too much.

Step 5: Choose Water Plants

Select water plants that vary in form, texture, color, and size. Group plants at the garden center before you buy to see how they look together. There are three types of plants: edgers, plants that are submerged, and plants that float. Select one tall plant to add vertical interest. Line the perimeter of the box with trailing plants.

In this project, we planted moisture-loving plants (deer fern and blue-eyed grass) as well as plants that prefer drier conditions (stonecrop and houseleek). If mixing plants with different growing requirements, place them in containers and set them in the box. Otherwise, fill the garden section of the box with potting soil and choose plants with similar light and watering needs.

For the water garden, a floating plant, such as duckweed, creates texture. A potted dwarf cattail is ideal for miniature gardens; place it on a brick so it sits 2 inches below the water surface.

As a finishing flourish, add ornamental elements such as a glass gazing ball, a wrought-iron piece, or a small koi.

Globe Fountain

Set a soothing scene in the garden with this easy-to-make and inexpensive terra-cotta fountain. Nothing soothes the senses in the garden quite like the sound of flowing water. You don't have to buy an expensive fountain to savor its relaxing melody. Create your own natural-looking water feature using inexpensive materials.

Time Required

1 to 2 hours

Supplies Needed

16-inch-diameter, 7-inch-tall terra-cotta bowl with drainage hole in bottom

Pond liner (available at home improvement stores)

9-inch-wide terra-cotta or glazed ceramic saucer

Small grounded submersible pump capable of pumping 60–80 gallons per hour

Flexible plastic tubing

Bag of rounded pebbles (¼- to ½-inch)

8- to 9-inch terra-cotta sphere (make sure it is high-fired or it will disintegrate when exposed to water)

String

Heavy-duty shears

Drill

Carbide-tip, masonry, or diamond drill bit (slightly larger than tubing)

Goggles

Bucket to wash gravel

Step 1: Cut Pond Liner

Using the string, measure the distance from the top edge of the terra-cotta bowl across the bottom to the top of the other side, allowing the string to conform to the shape of the bowl. Cut a piece of pond liner to a diameter slightly larger than that measurement. Place the liner in the bowl, slightly higher than the top. Avoid trimming the excess until the fountain is assembled.

Step 2: Position Saucer

Set the saucer upside down on the liner in the bottom of the terra-cotta bowl. Make sure the pump will fit under the saucer with the liner in place. Remove the saucer and drill several holes in the bottom to allow for good drainage. Drill one hole in the center large enough to accommodate the plastic tubing and one on the edge to allow clearance for the pump cord.

Step 3: Drill Hole

Using a drill bit slightly larger than the diameter of the plastic tubing, drill a hole in the top center of the sphere. Wear goggles for protection when using the drill; small terra-cotta chips tend to fly when the drill is operating.

Step 4: Position Tubing

Push one end of the tubing through the hole in the top of the sphere. Place the saucer upside down, then feed the other end of the tubing down through the hole in the center of the saucer, being careful not to pull it loose from the sphere.

Step 5: Connect Tubing

Center the sphere on the upside-down saucer. Connect the tubing coming from the saucer to the pump outlet and set everything back into the bowl. Bring the tubing straight up from the pump, through the saucer, and out the sphere top. Add water and test the pump. If everything works, trim the end of the plastic tubing flush with the bowl.

Step 6: Add Pebbles

Wash pebbles in a bucket of water to remove silt and grit, which can clog the pump. Fill the bowl with pebbles. Check the liner again to make sure it is evenly distributed throughout the bowl. There should be no low spots in any of the folds. Trim any excess to the top of the sphere. With use, the sphere will develop moss and take on a weathered look.

Millstone Fountain

Old-fashioned grindstones and an electric pump make a water feature that overflows with soothing sound.

Time Required

1 to 2 hours

Supplies Needed

Shallow round plastic liner
Soil
River rock or chipped brick
Board
Small recirculating pump
Two grindstones
Water
Mulch, rock, or spreading plants

MILLSTONES

Millstones are large round stones used in mills to grind wheat and other grains. They come in all sorts of sizes, from small to massive. Search salvage yards, flea markets, and landscaping companies for two grindstones that measure about 16 and 23 inches in diameter. There are also companies that create new millstones for garden use. Check local concrete fabricators for artisans in your area.

Step 1: Dig and Line a Hole
Purchase a shallow round liner slightly bigger than the large grindstone. The liner must be deep enough for the pump to be immersed. Dig a hole deep enough to sink the liner flush with the ground. Set the liner in the hole, make sure it is level, and add soil around it to hold it in place.

Step 2: Place the Pump
Set the water pump in the center of the liner. Place river rock or chipped brick under and around the pump, lifting it so it is about level with the top of the liner and securing it in place.

Step 3: Protect the Liner
Lay a board across the top of the liner. Mark the location where the board covers the pump and cut a hole the same size at that spot. Notch the ends of the board to set down over the liner; put it in place. The board will keep the stones above the edge of the liner.

Step 4: Stack the Grindstones
Position the grindstones over the board. Make sure all three holes line up. Fill the liner with water. Plug in the pump and adjust the flow. Conceal the ends of the board with mulch. The water supply will need to be replenished occasionally because of evaporation or runoff.

Beer-Tap Fountain

Add the soothing sound of water to your garden with a small fountain. A vintage beer tap is the centerpiece of this one. Look for beer taps at flea markets and tag sales. Keep in mind that the tap doesn't need to be in pristine condition—it will be out in the elements.

Time Required

1 to 2 hours

Supplies Needed

Vintage beer tap

Hacksaw

6-inch length of ½-inch-diameter rubber hose

Submersible pond pump (a 200- to 400-gallon-per-hour pump is sufficient)

Small hose clamp

Screwdriver

Three galvanized buckets

Six to eight large rocks

right A rustic fountain is the ideal focal point for a country garden.

Step 1: Shorten Tap and Cut Hose
Using a hacksaw, shorten the beer tap to the desired height. Our tap stands about 4 feet tall. Use the hacksaw to cut a 3-inch piece of rubber hose. The hose will connect the submersible pump and the beer tap. A clamp will hold the tap in place, making the connection watertight.

Step 2: Attach Hose to Pump
Place the rubber hose on the fountain portion of the submersible pump. It should fit snugly over the fountain spigot.

Step 3: Attach the Hose to the Tap
Slip a hose clamp over the rubber hose and insert the beer tap in the hose. Use a screwdriver to tighten the clamp.

Step 4: Add Pump to Bucket
Place the pump and attached beer tap in the bottom of a galvanized bucket. Position several large rocks around and on top of the pump to stabilize it in the bucket.

Step 5: Create a Base
Submerge one empty galvanized bucket upside down in the pond, filling it with water as you plunge it toward the bottom. The bucket will serve as a base for another empty galvanized bucket that will act as a catch basin for the fountain. Set the second empty bucket on top of the submerged bucket.

Step 6: Set the Beer Tap Pump
Place the galvanized bucket containing the beer tap, pump, and rocks in the pond, positioning it so the water from the beer tap will flow into the empty galvanized bucket. Plug in the fountain and enjoy.

Fountain in a Pot

One of the simplest water features you can make is a fountain in a terra-cotta container. So beautiful, so easy!

Time Required

1 to 2 hours

Supplies Needed

Container, 24 inches across or larger

Pump and fountain

Premixed quick-dry concrete

Liquid water sealant

Bricks

Outlet with ground fault circuit interrupter

FOCAL POINT

A fountain makes an ideal focal point for any garden. Many formal gardens feature a fountain at the center of a square or circular bed. If your garden is less formal, try a fountain in the center of a flowerbed set amid the blooms. Surrounding it with a mass of flowers is less structured, ideal for a country or cottage garden.

Step 1: Position the Pump
Using a pot that is at least 24 inches in diameter makes a splash and requires less water-refilling than a smaller pot. Pull the pump electrical cord through the drainage hole of the pot.

Step 2: Pull Out the Cord
Pull out enough cord to connect to the outlet—don't plug it in—and leave sufficient slack to raise the pump in the pot. Close the drainage hole with premixed quick-dry concrete. Let the concrete dry thoroughly; follow directions on the package.

Step 3: Seal the Inside of the Pot
Whether the container is terra-cotta, wood, or some other porous material, look for a liquid water sealant that is labeled for use on wood. Let the sealant dry completely.

Step 4: Elevate the Pump
Place the pump in the center of the container on bricks to bring it a few inches below where the water's surface will be. Fill the pot with water and connect the pump to the GFCI outlet. Be sure the water level does not dip below the pump.

Tub Water Garden

Thought you couldn't afford an elaborate water garden?
Craft this scaled-down version that's a snap to create.

Time Required

1 to 2 hours

Supplies Needed

Tublike container (we used a
  stainless-steel sitz bath)

Dechlorinator (available at
  aquatic supply stores)

Large stone or glass objects for
  accents

Water-garden plants

Fertilizer

Water creatures such as
  tadpoles and goldfish

Make a dramatic statement in your
landscape by fashioning a water garden
out of oak barrels, pots, old sinks, or—in
this case—an old stainless-steel tub. If
you opt for an oak barrel, you'll need to
line it with a polyvinyl chloride (PVC)
flexible liner in 20-mil thickness to keep
chemicals from leaching from the barrel
into the water.

For this simple (and inexpensive)
water-garden project, you can install
this great-looking pond and fill it with
water in a single afternoon, then launch
goldfish or koi into their new home about
48 hours later.

Step 1: Consider Your Site

Look for a spot that offers at least four hours of sun each day. Morning sun is kinder to water plants than late-day sun. Lay out your pond plan. In this project, we placed a variety of objects on the bottom of the pond. Some, such as inverted pots, serve as planting ledges for potted water plants. Other pieces of stone and terra-cotta provide interesting objects to spy through the water as well as places for tadpoles and fish to hide. Fill the pond with water and treat it with dechlorinator according to package directions.

Step 2: Add Flora

Your water-garden supplier can make suggestions about how many plants and animals your pond can adequately support. We added oxygenating grasses, water lilies, hornwort, and water hyacinths. Plant one bunch of oxygenating grasses per 2 square feet of pond surface; these grasses grow in containers sitting on the pond bottom. The water hyacinths float on the surface. The other plants are potted in pea gravel, but no soil, and are submerged in the water. Lilies grow best in pots submerged 6–10 inches below the surface.

Step 3: Keep It Clean

Wildlife such as tadpoles, goldfish, catfish, and snails will help keep your tank clean. Tadpoles clean up after the fish, fish eat insects, catfish eat algae off the bottom, and snails clean up the rest. If the balance is right, maintenance is simple. Experts suggest you add one snail and one fish per square foot of water surface area. To replace water due to evaporation, fill a bucket with water, treat the water with dechlorinator, and add to the pond after the water in the bucket becomes the same temperature as the pond water. Each day be sure to remove debris, spent blooms, and fallen leaves.

opposite A well-balanced aqua ecosystem can exist in a galvanized tub with the right mix of plants and water creatures.

Water Lily Potting

The water lily has cast its spell on humans for thousands of years, enchanting even the earliest civilizations. This mysterious beauty rises from the deep, leaves floating serenely on the surface, exquisite blossoms appearing as if by magic.

Time Required

1 to 2 hours

Supplies Needed

Planting container
Burlap
Heavy soil
Aquatic fertilizer
Pruners
Water lily tubers
Pea gravel

Water lilies, unlike some other water plants, need to be planted in soil. Growing lilies in a plastic-lined pond means that you need to pot them up and weight them down.

Hardy water lilies will survive the winter. Get them ready by removing dead and dying foliage. If the pond or water garden freezes solid in your climate or is drained for the winter, remove the lily, pot and all. Store the entire pot by keeping it cool and moist in a plastic bag. If you can't store the whole pot, remove and clean the growing tuber and store it in peat moss at 40–50°F.

If the pond doesn't freeze solid, don't remove the pot. Simply lower it to the deepest part of the pond, where water will not freeze.

In spring, bring the pot back to the proper growing level in the pond. If you've dug up and stored the tuber, repot as if it were a new plant.

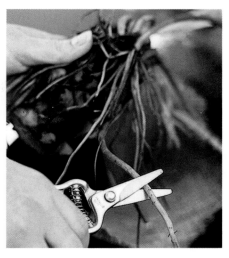

Step 1: Get a Container
Use a container that is wide and shallow. A good size is 12–18 inches wide by 6–10 inches deep. The tuber, which is similar to the rhizome of an iris, grows horizontally. Containers may or may not have holes. If there are drainage holes, line the pot with burlap to keep the soil in the container. Soil that leaches out can cloud the water in your pond.

Step 2: Add Heavy Soil
Use a heavy soil intended for use in the garden, not a fluffy potting soil that will float out of the container. Avoid soil mixes with perlite, vermiculite, or peat for the same reason. Enrich the soil with aquatic fertilizer pellets made especially for the task. Push them into the soil before you plant.

Step 3: Cut Off Dead Parts
Remove old leaves and thick, fleshy old roots. Leave only emerging leaves and buds and the newer, hairlike roots.

Step 4: Plant Water Lily Tubers
Plant the tuber against the side of the pot, with the growing tip pointing upward (about 45 degrees) and toward the center of the pot.

Step 5: Cover Soil with Stones
Cover the soil with a layer of rock or pea gravel to keep the soil in the pot.

Step 6: Place Pot in Water Garden
The planted pot should be lowered into the pond at an angle to allow air to escape. Set the base of the pot 12–18 inches deep. The leaves will float to the surface. If the pond is deeper than 18 inches and doesn't have built-in planting ledges, support the pot.

CHAPTER FOUR

Cool Containers

Overflowing with lush foliage and colorful flowers, containers are the easiest (and most beautiful) way to add color to your patio, porch, and garden.

Essence of Summer

A gorgeous orange container calls for a planting scheme that's hot, fun, and vibrant. Pair red, yellow, and orange flowers with sultry dark foliage.

Hot, hot, hot! That's the color scheme of this gorgeous container. Filled with red- and yellow-hue flowers and foliage, this combination shows that you can't go wrong with excess. The citrus-orange container is packed with tall to trailing varieties. The drama of the container is heightened by the large, striped leaves of 'Tropicanna' canna. This showy bulb produces huge leaves nonstop all summer. Hot red dahlias and sizzling red ornamental peppers turn up the heat in this sun-loving container. It's perfect for poolside, on patios, or sunny porches.

Plant List

A. 'Tropicanna' Canna
(*Canna*) Zones 9–11

B. 'Blackie' Sweet Potato Vine
(*Ipomoea batatas*) Annual

C. 'Bishop of Llandaff' Dahlia
(*Dahlia*) Zones 8–10

D. 'Lucky Red Flame' Lantana
(*Lantana*) Zones 9–11

E. Ornamental Red Pepper
(*Capsicum*) Annual

F. Orange-Golden Red-Hot Poker
(*Kniphofia*) Zones 5–9

G. 'Kaleidoscope' Abelia
(*Abelia* × *grandiflora*) Zones 6–9

H. 'Illumination' Vinca
(*Vinca minor*) Zones 4–10

'Tropicanna' Canna

'Blackie' Sweet Potato Vine

'Bishop of Llandaff' Dahlia

'Lucky Red Flame' Lantana

Ornamental Red Pepper

Red-Hot Poker

'Kaleidoscope' Abelia

'Illumination' Vinca

Lush and Leafy

Create a leafy garden paradise in a pot with an all-foliage combination that looks wildly colorful even in the shade.

Time Required

2 to 4 hours

Supplies Needed

Container: 16 inches wide by 19 inches tall

Exposure

Full to part afternoon shade

Here's an easy-to-replicate design tip: Repeat leaf shapes in a container to create continuity. This dramatic green, purple, and white combination is all dependent on the drama that foliage plants deliver. The large leaves of caladium are so showy and colorful. Their heart-shape foliage is available in a wide range of colorful options, so using this heat-loving plant in containers is a smart idea. Coleus is another colorful foliage plant that offers a wide range of color options. Because this container features shade-lovers, using a large, dramatic ghost fern as the vertical element is possible. Ghost fern is silver in spring; fronds deepen to grayish-green as temperatures rise during the summer.

Plant List

A. Caladium Bicolors
   (*Caladium*) Zones 10–11

B. Calathea
   (*Calathea roseo picta*) Houseplant

C. 'Magilla' Perilla
   (*Solenostemon* hybrids) Annual

D. Ghost Fern
   (*Athyrium* 'Ghost') Zones 3–8

Caladium

Calathea

'Magilla' Perilla

'Ghost' Fern

BHG TEST GARDEN TIP

COOL CALADIUM

Providing color pizzazz in dim places where flowers can't, caladiums have come into their own recently with the craze for tropical plants. The clumping, heart-shape leaves are available in a variety of veined patterns in colors from cream to neon pinks, reds, silvers, and greens. Newer introductions bring caladiums out of the shade. The more substantial leaves of the Florida series, with greater heat tolerance, give the splashy caladiums their place in the sun. Plant caladium tubers shallowly in pots and water sparingly until sprouts appear. They begin to grow vigorously once the weather warms in late spring to early summer.

Colorful Combos

Mix it up! Don't be afraid to combine perennials, annuals, and houseplants to create the colorful look you want.

Time Required

2 to 4 hours

Supplies Needed

Container: 14 inches wide by 14 inches tall

Exposure

Morning sun, afternoon shade

This brilliant cobalt blue pot features an oakleaf croton as the design's upright element. Echoing the carnival colors of the croton is a glorious mix of New Guinea impatiens and lemony-yellow begonias.

Foliage also plays an important role in this container's stunning success, with the two-tone bronze sweet potato vine providing a lovely cascading effect over top of the container.

Add bright accents of color with coralbells, also called heuchera. This perennial is known more for its foliage than flowers. Heucheras come in a wide range of colors and make excellent pot companions with colorful flowers.

This eye-catching container doesn't shy away from combining a lot of elements and a lot of color.

Croton

New Guinea Impatiens

Rieger Begonia

Heuchera

Bronze Sweet Potato Vine

Sundew Springs Lysimachia

Plant List

A. Croton
(*Codiaeum variegatum pictum*)
Houseplant

B. New Guinea Impatiens
(*Impatiens hawkeri*) Annual

C. Rieger Begonia
(*Begonia × hiemalis*) Annual

D. Coralbells
(*Heuchera villosa*) Zones 3–9

E. Bronze Sweet Potato Vine
(*Ipomoea batatas*) Annual

F. Sundew Springs Lysimachia
(*Lysimachia* hybrid) Zones 9–11

BHG TEST GARDEN TIP
COLORFUL CROTON

Croton is a colorful shrub with leathery leaves that are most colorful in bright light. In low-light conditions, new leaves will be smaller and less intensely pigmented. Grow croton at 60–85°F with high humidity. Allow the soil surface to dry between waterings. Use this beautiful houseplant in summer patio containers, then bring it indoors and enjoy it as a houseplant in winter.

Modern Twist

Purple and chartreuse make great planting partners with a modern twist. Add a fantastic fan palm to make this container a real standout.

Time Required

2 to 4 hours

Supplies Needed

Container: 22 inches long by 11 inches wide by 16 inches tall

Exposure

Full sun

This rich, shiny burgundy oval-shape pot looks stunning with an asymmetrical emphasis. Although the footprint of the pot is small, it looks large because of its width. The side placement of the dramatic windmill palm and the echoing spikiness of the phormium make this container a study in texture and color.

The grape-purple heliotrope is always a smart choice for containers. It has a distinctive scent—some say it smells like cherry pie; others say a grape Popsicle. Still others say it's reminiscent of vanilla. Regardless, it is undeniably one of the most intriguingly scented plants in the garden. As a bonus, this tropical plant, grown as an annual, bears big clusters of rich purple, blue, or white flowers.

Windmill Palm

New Zealand Flax

Lemon Coral Sedum

Superbells Calibrachoa

Coprosma

Heliotrope

Plant List

A. Windmill Palm
(*Trachycarpus fortunei*) Zones 8–11

B. New Zealand Flax
(*Phormium*) Zones 4–9

C. Lemon Coral Sedum
(*Sedum rupestre*) Annual

D. Superbells Yellow Calibrachoa
(*Calibrachoa*) Annual

E. 'Rainbow Surprise' Coprosma
(*Coprosma*) Zones 9–10

F. 'Fragrant Delight' Heliotrope
(*Heliotropium*) Annual

BHG TEST GARDEN TIP

NEW ZEALAND FLAX

Bring a note of the tropics to your garden with the bold, colorful, strappy leaves of New Zealand flax. They are excellent as container plants that can be overwintered with protection, but in warm areas, they're spectacular planted directly in the ground. Flower panicles may reach 12 feet tall in some selections, with red or yellow tubular flowers. Blooms appear only in mild climates, but there they attract many species of birds. If space is limited, check out dwarf forms. While New Zealand flax is a popular perennial in frost-free areas, it's becoming more and more loved in northern regions, where it's treated as an annual.

Cool in the Shade

Fantastic foliage is the key to this design. The palmleaf begonia luxurians can be brought indoors as a houseplant at the end of the season.

Time Required

2 to 4 hours

Supplies Needed

Container: 16 inches wide by 19 inches tall

Exposure

Full sun

Gardeners can enjoy a tropical-inspired garden no matter where they live by choosing plants that are big, bold, and eye-catching. Go for lush and abundant by adding a dramatic focal plant such as a large palmleaf begonia luxurians, a banana tree, a palm, or a fern.

With a strong focal point, every other plant decision is related to that key plant. In this container, the umbrellalike foliage of the palmleaf begonia luxurians is the main event. The pops of color from the variegated-leaf, upright New Guinea impatiens contrasts nicely with the flowing chartreuse leaves of the golden creeping Jenny.

Although this container has just three types of plants, it appears lush and complex. And beautiful!

Plant List

A. Palmleaf Begonia Luxurians
(*Begonia luxurians*) Zones 8–11

B. Golden Creeping Jenny
(*Lysimachia nummularia*) Zones 4–8

C. 'Painted Paradise Red' New Guinea Impatiens
(*Impatiens hawkeri*) Zones 5–10

Palmleaf Begonia Luxurians

Golden Creeping Jenny

New Guinea Impatiens

BHG TEST GARDEN TIP

GOLDEN CREEPING JENNY

Lysimachia nummularia 'Aurea' is a fast-growing groundcover for shade or partial shade. It bears round chartreuse foliage and grows 2 inches tall. It can spread indefinitely, which makes it an attractive addition to containers. Use this perennial in window boxes to attain a beautiful cascading effect. If you want to keep it from year to year, plant creeping jenny in the ground to overwinter. You can use it in containers the following year. In some climates, it can survive happily in its container over the winter.

Dynamic Duo

A pair of cubes in refreshing turquoise and chartreuse calls for restraint when it comes to plant selection. Showy foliage plants, such as dracaena and taro, make bold statements without being colorful.

Time Required

2 to 4 hours

Supplies Needed

Container: 16 inches wide by 19 inches tall; 13 inches wide by 16 inches tall

Exposure

Morning sun, afternoon shade

Two are better than one when it comes to containers. Pairing pots and mixing foliage allows you to create a bigger impression. In this daring duo, the pots are the colorful elements while the plants are more subdued. Yet there's a lot going on: structure, texture, and a controlled color palette.

The chartreuse container plays the color card with a mix of 'Lemon Lime' dracaena (a houseplant!) that echoes the color in the container. The soft white impatiens adds pops of brightness.

The turquoise container uses big-leaf taro to make a big impact. This tropical beauty grows fast in summer's heat. Taro's dark purple leaves pick up color from the purple veins in the coleus, and the wire vine adds a little flouncy flourish over the sides of the container.

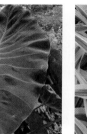
Black Taro

'Lemon Lime' Dracaena

'Gay's Delight' Coleus

Wire Vine

'Sweet Caroline' Sweet Potato Vine

Impatiens

Plant List

A. **'Jet Black Wonder' Black Taro**
(*Colocasia*) Zones 7–11

B. **'Lemon Lime' Dracaena**
(*Dracaena deremensis*) Zones 10–11

C. **'Gay's Delight' Coleus**
(*Solenostemon* hybrids) Annual

D. **Wire Vine**
(*Muehlenbeckia axillaris*) Zones 3–10

E. **'Sweet Caroline' Sweet Potato Vine**
(*Ipomoea batatas*) Annual

F. **White Impatiens**
(*Impatiens walleriana*) Annual

BHG TEST GARDEN TIP

TERRIFIC TARO

This leafy lovely goes by several names: taro, elephant's ears, and colocasia. This lush, tropical accent looks good in any climate. Elephant's ears are hardier than their close relatives (alocasias), and their leaves are heart-shape and larger. When summer's warm weather arrives, they grow fast, achieving a large spread of at least 5 feet. Colocasias languish in drought but thrive in wet soils.

Exotic Statement

Think big and bold by adding a red-leaf banana plant to a big, bold container. It loves hot summer weather and will grow just like it does in the tropics.

Time Required

2 to 4 hours

Supplies Needed

Container: 16 inches wide by 19 inches tall

Exposure

Full sun

What's more tropical than a banana? Gardeners in every climate (not just the tropics) can grow this beauty in a container. The red-leaf variety has it all: height, color, and lush leaves. This large plant rises above the rest of the colorful mix. The two colors of sweet potato vine (chartreuse and black) offer balance to the container with their equally vivacious growth. These vigorous trailing vines will pour over the container's edge, sometimes even flowing across the ground around the planter. Lush and luscious!

Plant List

A. Red Banana
(*Musa sumatrana*) Zones 8–11

B. Heliotrope
(*Heliotropium*) Annual

C. Kalanchoe
(*Kalanchoe blossfeldiana*) Annual

D. Bonfire Begonia
(*Begonia boliviensis*) Annual

E. 'Blackie' Sweet Potato Vine
(*Ipomoea batatas*) Annual

F. 'Marguerite' Sweet Potato Vine
(*Ipomoea batatas*) Annual

Red Banana

Heliotrope

Kalanchoe

'Bonfire' Begonia

'Blackie' Sweet Potato Vine

'Marguerite' Sweet Potato Vine

BHG TEST GARDEN TIP — SWEET POTATO VINE

Among the most popular container-garden plants, sweet potato vine is a vigorous grower that you can count on to make a big impact. Its colorful foliage, in shades of chartreuse or purple, accents just about any other plant. Grow a few together in a large pot and they make a big impact all on their own. Sweet potato vines do best during the warm days of summer and prefer moist, well-drained soil. They thrive in sun or shade.

Big Shots

Who needs flowers when foliage looks this lush and showy? There's nothing subtle about this container, even though the color scheme is toned down. Combine houseplants with annuals to create beautiful potted gardens with staying power.

Time Required

2 to 4 hours

Supplies Needed

Container: 16 inches tall

Exposure

Partial sun/partial shade

A group of leafy common houseplants, including *Plectranthus*, airplane plant, *Tradescantia*, and *Peperomia*, take their act to a partially sunny stage. These plants will triple in size over the summer, thanks to the tropical temperatures and humidity. The houseplants and annuals, some trailing and others compact, unite in their common color scheme: purple with white details. When the cold temperatures arrive in autumn, simply lift the houseplants from the container and repot indoors.

Airplane Plant

Peek-A-Boo

Tahitian Bridal Veil

Peperomia

Tradescantia zebrina

'Sassy White' Marguerite Daisy

'Mona Lavender' Plectranthus

Plant List

A. Airplane Plant
   (*Chlorophytum comosum*) Houseplant

B. Peek-A-Boo
   (*Spilanthes oleracea*) Annual

C. Tahitian Bridal Veil
   (*Tradescantia multiflora*) Houseplant

D. Peperomia
   (*Peperomia caperata*) Houseplant

E. Tradescantia zebrina
   (*Tradescantia zebrina*) Houseplant

F. 'Sassy White' Marguerite Daisy
   (*Argyranthemum frutescens*) Annual

G. 'Mona Lavender' Plectranthus
   (*Plectranthus*) Zones 10–11

Think Pink

A single-color theme makes planting easy. Pink links each plant in this grouping, in foliage or flowers, creating a vibrant display for a shaded location.

Time Required
2 to 4 hours
Supplies Needed
Container: 12 inches tall
Exposure
Shade

Using tropical houseplants in outdoor containers is a great way to stretch your budget. Just move your houseplants outdoors, combining them into groupings with other houseplants and colorful annuals. In this planter, three popular houseplants (snakeplant, polka-dot plant, and Madagascar dragon tree) rub shoulders with some pink-hue colorful characters: impatiens and begonias. These standup annuals do well in shaded areas, the same type of light needed for the houseplants. They make beautiful music together. Plus, your houseplants will love a summer outdoors in the fresh air. They'll look refreshed and revived when you take them indoors at the end of summer.

Snakeskin Plant

Polka-Dot Plant

Tuberous Begonia

Madagascar Dragon Tree

Coral Impatiens

Plant List

A. Snakeskin Plant
(*Fittonia argyroneura*) Houseplant

B. Polka-Dot Plant
(*Hypoestes phyllostachy*) Annual

C. Tuberous Begonia
(*Begonia × tuberhybrida*) Annual

D. Madagascar Dragon Tree
(*Dracaena marginata*) Houseplant

E. Coral Impatiens
(*Impatiens walleriana*) Annual

BHG TEST GARDEN TIP

PINK IT UP

Pink flowers add a bold or delicate touch to the garden, depending on which shades you use. Use light pink flowers for an airy feel or bright pink flowers that pop against a green background.

Rising Stars

A fountain of burgundy foliage rises from a burgundy-red container. Trailing begonias intertwined with asparagus ferns create a lovely "skirt" of flowers and foliage. This easy combination features just four types of plants, yet feels so lush and diverse.

Time Required

2 to 4 hours

Supplies Needed

Container: 17 inches tall

Exposure

Partial sun

A supporting cast of asparagus ferns with Bellfire and Bonfire begonias highlights the deserving diva of the container: the showy cordyline. 'Red Star' and 'Dark Star' cordylines make ideal container stars because they offer dramatic color and a lovely fountain of spiky foliage. The combination of tall, spiky plants with trailing ones is unbeatable. Consider the growth habit of plants as well as their color and foliage texture when pairing them up. The begonias will bloom happily all summer.

Plant List

A. **Cordyline**
   (*Cordyline australis*) Zones 9–10

B. **Asparagus Fern**
   (*Asparagus densiflorus* 'Sprengeri')
   Annual

C. **Bonfire Begonia**
   (*Begonia boliviensis* Bonfire)
   Annual

D. **Bellfire Begonia**
   (*Begonia boliviensis* Bellfire)
   Annual

Cordyline

Asparagus Fern

'Bellfire' Begonia

'Bonfire' Begonia

BEAUTIFUL BEGONIA

(BHG TEST GARDEN TIP)

Talk about foolproof: Annual begonia is about as easy as it gets. It does well in a variety of conditions, but to keep begonia its most luxuriant best, give it light shade; rich, well-drained soil; and ample water. It also loves plenty of fertilizer, so be generous. Plant annual begonias in spring after all danger of frost has passed. No need to deadhead this flower unless you want to—it's "self-cleaning!"

Continuous Color

Plant a container that won't disappoint—from spring through fall. This colorful combination relies on the terrific talents of coleus, a plant with many personalities and colors.

Time Required
2 to 4 hours
Supplies Needed
Container: 14 inches tall
Exposure
Partial shade

This mostly leafy ensemble stars a stunning duo of coleus varieties and performs a nonstop show in partial shade. For best results, take coleus cuttings in late summer, poke the cut ends into small containers of potting mix, and overwinter them indoors. The next generation of plants will be well-developed and ready for potting outdoors in spring. Try red-hue coleus varieties such as 'Solar Eclipse' and 'Redhead'.

Plant List

A. Red Coleus
(*Solnostemon scutellarioides*) Annual

B. Variegated Duranta
(*Duranta erecta*) Zones 8–11

C. 'Cooler Raspberry' Vinca
(*Catharanthus roseus*) Annual

D. Beefsteak Plant
(*Iresine*) Annual

E. 'Magenta Moon' Torenia
(*Torenia hybrid*) Annual

F. 'Lava Rose' Coleus
(*Solenostemon scutellarioides*) Annual

G. English Ivy
(*Hedera helix*) Zones 5–9

Red Coleus

Variegated Duranta

'Cooler Raspberry' Vinca

Beefsteak Plant

'Magenta Moon' Torenia

'Lava Rose' Coleus

English Ivy

CHAPTER FIVE

Super Structures

Add architectural interest to your yard and garden with trellises, towers, and tepees.

If you can't find new timbers with the exact dimensions of existing timbers, it might be best to remove additional timbers so you can create an entire new section or more easily restart a running pattern such as this stairstep design.

Timber Wall Replacement

Split, rotting landscape timbers are unsightly, and they can attract home-damaging pests such as carpenter ants and termites.

Replacing old and rotting landscape timbers is relatively inexpensive and fairly easy for a handy homeowner. Most timber walls shorter than 36 inches can repaired using simple tools and the steps shown here. For walls taller than 36 inches and those holding back potentially active grades—such as those next to a driveway, below a sidewalk, or against a steep slope—discuss repairs with a landscaping or construction professional. If your repairs include digging in previously undisturbed soil, locate underground utilities before work begins.

above Wall before replacement.

Timber Wall Replacement

Time Required

1 to 2 days

Supplies Needed

Electric saw
Electric drill
Crowbar
6- or 8-inch timber screws
4- or 6-foot timbers

Step 1: Locate and Cut Rods
You'll know it's time to replace your timber retaining walls when they start to crack and collapse. Locate steel rods or spikes that fasten existing timbers by sliding a thin metal blade, such as an old kitchen knife, between joints. Cut rods or spikes using a reciprocating saw fitted with a metal cutting blade.

Step 2: Pry Timbers Apart
Use a crowbar to pry the timbers apart. Remove damaged timbers.

Step 3: Make Fresh Cuts Use old timbers as templates for angles and lengths. Mark cut lines on all four sides of timbers to keep your cuts as square as possible. Use a tree-pruning blade in a reciprocating saw or a bow saw to cut new timbers.

Step 4: Gather Proper Gear
Make sure you have an electric drill and matching hex socket (usually included in packages of timber screws) and specially designed timber screws—self-starting, slender-shank hardened-steel screws with hex heads.

Step 5: Drill Timbers
Join new timbers to each other and to any remaining sound timbers by driving screw heads flush or slightly below the surface of timbers.

Step 6: Preserve It
Some manufacturers of pressure-treated timbers recommend treating site-cut ends with an additional application of preservative. Ask your lumber sales associate whether that is required for your timbers.

TIMBER TIPS

With the right equipment, replacing timbers can be a satisfying project.

- Although most cordless drills can drive timber screws, some timbers may require the extra power and torque of a corded drill, depending on the screw length, wood species, timber thickness, and amount of liquid preservative remaining in the timber fibers.

- Use 6-inch screws with 4-inch timbers; 8-inch screws with 6-inch timbers. Drive screws through new timbers into timber below every 18–24 inches; start screws about 4 inches in from ends. Use one-size smaller screws to pull faces of mitered timbers together.

- Actual timber sizes are nominal, or approximate (a timber labeled 6-inch, for example, may actually measure only 5½ inches).

- You might not find new timbers with exact dimensions of existing timbers. In that case, it may be best to remove additional existing timbers to create an entire "new" section or more easily restart a running pattern.

- Specify "ground contact" when purchasing pressure-treated timbers.

Copper Obelisk

Beautiful copper is a hot—and pricey—commodity in garden ornaments. But you can assemble this obelisk with inexpensive parts.

All the materials needed for this garden classic are routinely stocked at hardware stores. Fittings are less expensive if you can find contractor packs of 10 or more to a bag. Copper pipe is often sold in lengths of 10 feet, so three 10-foot lengths should do. However, you'll need nearly all of 30 feet for this project, so be sure to cut the longer pieces first, then use the leftovers for the shorter pieces. Pipe cutters come in a range of sizes and prices. Many general-purpose glues should work; just be sure the label says it is suitable for metal. Epoxy glues may be used, but you'll need one that is slow to harden: a half hour or more.

Time Required

1 to 2 hours

Supplies Needed

30 feet ½-inch straight copper pipe

32 ½-inch copper tees

4 ½-inch copper 45-degree elbows

2 ½-inch copper 90-degree elbows

4 ½-inch copper pipe caps

Tape measure or ruler

Felt-tip marker

Handheld pipe cutter

Glue suitable for metal

Cloth rag

3 large rubber bands

opposite This sturdy structure can handle lightweight climbers such as clematis or heavier vines such as roses.

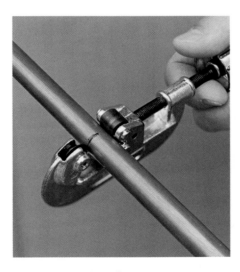

MEASUREMENTS FOR COPPER PIECES

8 @ 7 inches
4 @ 7¼ inches
4 @ 8 inches
4 @ 8¾ inches
4 @ 9½ inches
12 @ 12 inches
18 @ 1 inch
2 @ 2 inches

Step 1: Cut the Pieces

You'll need the quantities and lengths of ½-inch copper pipe indicated *above right*. Minor variances (less than ⅛ inch) are tolerable, but the more precise your measurements are, the better the final product. With the 1-inch pieces, do not exceed 1 inch even by a small amount or the pieces will not fit completely in the tee fittings, leaving visible gaps. For each piece, measure the length and mark the cutting point on the pipe with a felt-tip marker. Cut at that point with the pipe cutter. The pipe cutter uses a scoring wheel that cuts the pipe as you rotate the cutter. You simply insert the pipe, tighten the clamp, and turn. It normally takes just a few rotations of the cutter to complete the cut. The cut ends can be sharp, so be careful.

Copper Obelisk

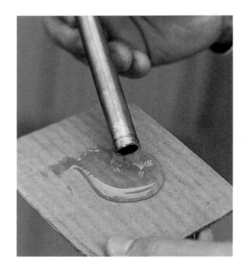

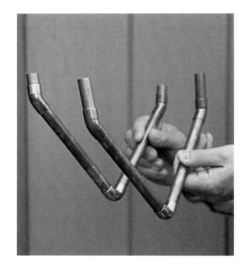

Step 2: Assemble the Obelisk

After you cut the pipe pieces, assemble the obelisk without glue to make sure it goes together as planned. If it looks like it will work, disassemble it in reverse order, being sure to keep the pieces laid out in the same sequence so they'll be organized when you put them back together. When you're ready for the final assembly, squeeze glue onto a piece of cardboard and dip the pipe ends into it before inserting them into their fittings. Use a cloth rag to clean up excess glue. The glue will remain soft long enough for assembly. Though the glue doesn't need to form a perfect seal, you want it to be reasonably strong, so be sure you get glue around the entire circumference of each pipe end. Press each end firmly into its fitting to ensure sturdy construction. The obelisk consists of four tiers of horizontal rungs connected by vertical pieces. It stands on four legs and is capped with a peak.

Step 3: Build the Sections

Put together the corners of the first tier. Each corner consists of two tees joined by a 1-inch connector. The tees should be offset 90 degrees. Use four 9½-inch pieces (rungs) to connect the corners, forming a square. Insert four 7-inch pieces into the tier's bottom openings for legs; place caps on the other ends.

Insert four 12-inch pieces into the first tier's top openings. Assemble a second tier, using 8¾-inch lengths for rungs. Place that square atop the 12-inch vertical pieces.

Insert four more 12-inch vertical pieces into the second tier's top openings. Assemble the third tier as you did the first two. Place the square atop the just-inserted vertical pieces.

Insert the last four 12-inch pieces into the third tier's top openings. Assemble the fourth and final tier using 7¼-inch lengths for rungs; place the square on top of the just-inserted vertical pieces.

Step 4: Make the Peaks

Construct the two peak assemblies, each using two 7-inch pieces joined by a 90-degree elbow. Insert a 45-degree elbow on the other end of each 7-inch piece.

Step 5: Top It Off

Finish the obelisk by joining the peak assemblies to the top tier. Place one 1-inch connector into each of the 45-degree elbows of one peak assembly. Set the assembly in place atop the obelisk by inserting the connectors into the tees at opposite corners of the top tier. Repeat this step with the other peak assembly, using a 2-inch connector in each elbow to join it to the remaining two corner fittings. This peak piece will sit slightly above the first. Once completed, view it from several angles, adjusting it as necessary to get a symmetrical appearance. Large rubber bands placed around the structure may help hold it rigid until the glue dries (allow 24 hours).

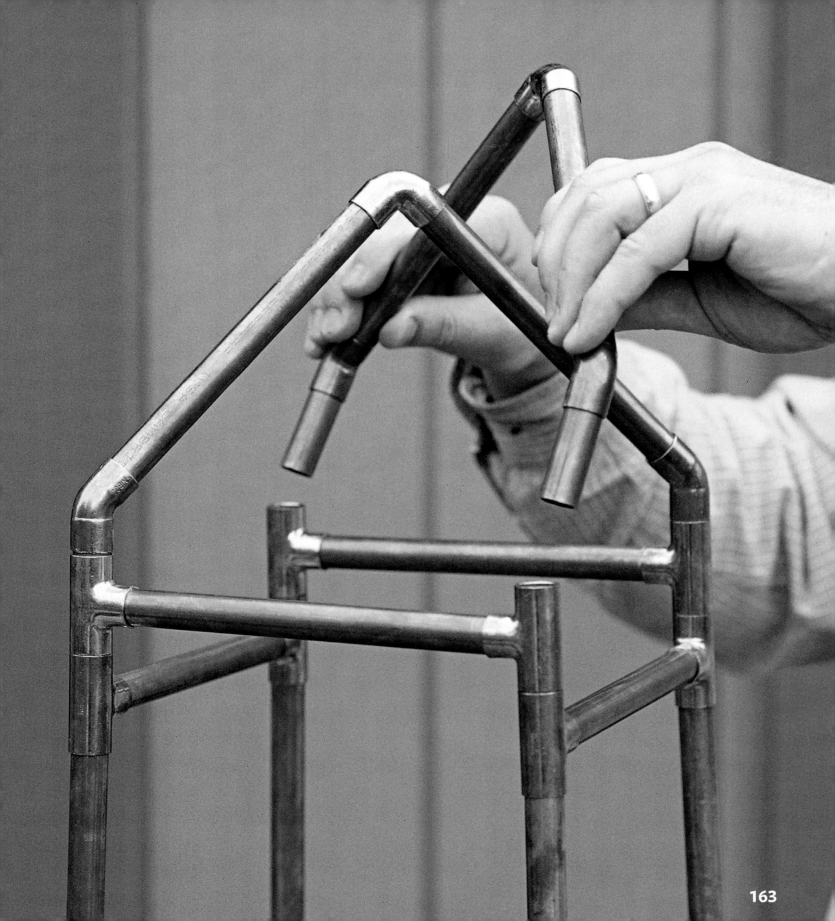

A garden tuteur (with planting container) is an ideal project for a small-space garden or narrow patio because of its small footprint.

Flower-Tower Tuteur

Build a sturdy and beautiful pyramid for your garden or front entryway. This classic structure looks good with vines climbing on the outside and plants inside the structure.

Create a beautiful garden focal point and give climbing plants an upscale home with this geometric gem. The roughly 50-inch-tall tuteur can be used freestanding or in a container. *Tuteur* is a French word meaning guardian or tutor. It also describes structures or props used to "tutor," or train, climbing plants. Tuteurs aren't new. They're based on designs found in European gardens as early as the 17th century.

Time Required

1 to 2 days

Supplies Needed

- Wood (see dimensions, *right*)
- #18×¾-inch galvanized nails
- #8×1½-inch stainless-steel flathead wood screws
- Spray adhesive
- Exterior-type adhesive
- Sander
- Clamps
- Table saw
- Wood glue
- Bandsaw
- Plane
- Drill

MATERIALS LIST (All dimensions in inches)

Part	T	W	L	Matl.	Qty.
A* legs	1	1	47	C	4
B* rail blanks	¼	1	22	C	4
C* rail blanks	¼	1	5	C	4
D* rail blanks	¼	1	18	C	4
E* rail blanks	¼	1	14	C	4
F* rail blanks	¼	1	10	C	4
G vertical trim	⅛	1½	32	C	4
H base	½	3¾	3¾	C	1
I cap	½	2½	2½	C	1
J finial	1½	1½	6	C	1
K mounting blocks	¾	¾	3½	C	2

*Parts initially cut oversize. See the instructions.
Materials key: C=cedar

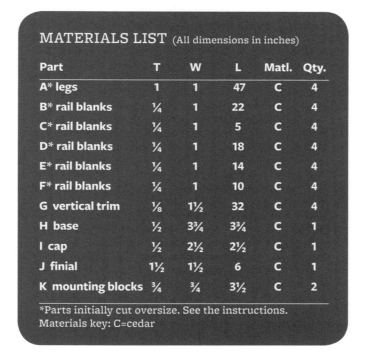

A*
A*
1½" x 5½" x 48"Cedar (2x6)
*F
*E
*C
*D
*B
1½" x 5½" x 24"Cedar (2x6)
*Plane or resaw to the thickness listed in the supply list.
J
*K
G
1½" x 3½" x 32"Cedar (2x4)
*H
*I
¾" x 5½" x 12"Cedar (1x6)

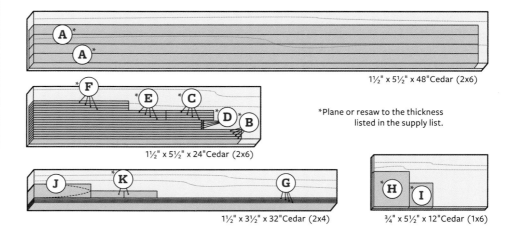

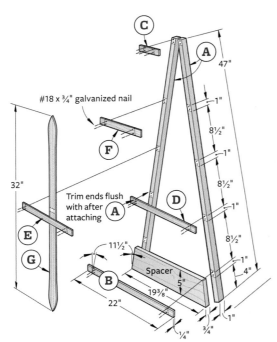

#18 x ¾" galvanized nail

Trim ends flush
with after
attaching

Drawing 1

Construct the Sides (Photo A)

Assemble the Sides (Photo B)

Step 1: Cut the Lumber

From a 48-inch 2×6 cedar board planed to 1 inch thick, cut the legs (A) to the size indicated in the Materials List, *page 165*. Mark the locations for the rail blanks (B, D, E, F) on the legs, where dimensioned on Drawing 1, *above*.

Plane a 24-inch 2×6 cedar board to 1 inch thick. Rip 16 ¼-inch-thick, 1-inch-wide strips from the edge of the board for the rail blanks (B through F), referring to Drawing 3, *opposite*, for layout. Crosscut the strips to the listed lengths.

From scrap ¾-inch plywood, make a 5×19⅜-inch spacer and miter-cut its ends at 11½ degrees, where shown on Drawing 1.

Step 2: Construct the Sides

Lay two legs (A) on your workbench with the markings visible and position the spacer between them with the bottom edges flush. Clamp the legs to the spacer.

Glue and nail a rail blank (B) to the legs, where shown on Drawing 1, aligning it with the marks and roughly centering it end to end. Use an exterior-type adhesive, such as Titebond II or polyurethane glue. In the same way, attach a rail blank (C) to the legs with the top edges flush and the legs 3 inches apart at the rail's bottom edge, where shown on Drawing 2, *below*. Attach the other rail blanks (D, E, F) to the legs. When the glue dries, trim the rails' ends flush with the legs' outside edges, as shown in Photo A, *above*.

Step 3: Assemble the Sides

From a 32-inch 2×4 cedar board, rip four ⅛-inch-thick, 1½-inch-wide strips for the vertical trim (G). Face-join the strips using a few pieces of double-face tape. Make two copies of the Finial Diagram, *opposite*.

Adhere the patterns to the ends of a strip and draw lines to connect them, where shown on Drawing 3. Cut the strips to shape and sand the curved edges smooth. Carefully separate the strips and remove the tape.

Glue a vertical trim strip (G) to the side assembly, where shown on Drawings 1 and 3. Center it side to side in the assembly with an equal overhang above rail F and below rail D. Note that the trim fits behind rail E and in front of rails D and F.

Repeat the process to assemble the opposing side.

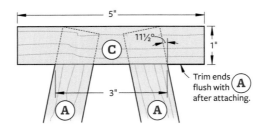

Trim ends flush with (A) after attaching.

Drawing 2

Assemble the Top (Photo C)

Drawing 3

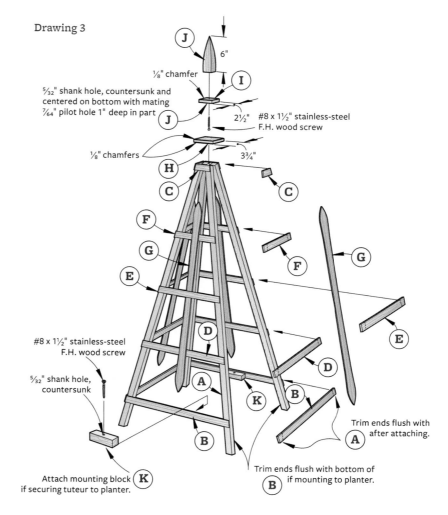

⅛" chamfer

⁵⁄₃₂" shank hole, countersunk and centered on bottom with mating ⁷⁄₆₄" pilot hole 1" deep in part **J**

6"

⅛" chamfers

2½"   #8 x 1½" stainless-steel F.H. wood screw

3¾"

#8 x 1½" stainless-steel F.H. wood screw

⁵⁄₃₂" shank hole, countersunk

Trim ends flush with after attaching. **A**

Attach mounting block **K** if securing tuteur to planter.

Trim ends flush with bottom of **B** if mounting to planter.

Step 4: Assemble the Tower

Position the two side assemblies upright and opposite each other. As shown in Photo B, clamp the spacer between the assemblies and attach the rail blanks (B through F) to the legs in the same order as before. (A power nailer is ideal for this.) Repeat the process on the opposite side. Trim the rails' ends and install the remaining vertical trim (G).

From a 12-inch 1×6 cedar board planed to ½ inch thick, cut the base (H) and cap (I) to the sizes listed. Chamfer their edges, where shown on Drawing 3.

Step 5: Make the Finial

Cut the finial (J) to the dimensions listed. Make two copies of the Finial Diagram. Adhere one pattern to the finial. Cut to the pattern lines. Adhere the other pattern to one of the curved sides and cut again. Sand the finial smooth.

Center and glue the finial to the top of the cap (I). Drill a pilot and countersunk shank hole through the bottom of the cap, where shown, and drive the screw. Center and glue this assembly to the base (H).

Sand the top of the tuteur flat, as shown in Photo C, *above*. Then center, glue, and clamp the top assembly (H, I, J) to the rails (C).

Finial Diagram

G

PATTERN FOR VERTICAL TRIM AND FINIAL (2 needed)

5"

1⅛"
³⁄₁₆"   ³⁄₁₆"
1½"

Bentwood Tepee

This twiggy tepee, known in garden circles as a tuteur, guides and supports plants. This willow tepee makes a beautiful garden focal point, even when it's not supporting a climbing plant. Crafted from flexible willow trimmings, this tepee can be made in one afternoon.

Time Required

2 to 4 hours

Supplies Needed

8 willow posts, 7–8 feet long,
1½ inches in diameter

25 feet of 14-gauge wire

Metal macrame ring (or other
type of ring), 18-inch diameter

50 thin willow rods, 5–6 feet long

Eight 1-inch brown ring-shank
panel nails

Hammer

Step 1: Obtain Fresh Willow
Gather eight willow posts. Strip off the leaves. About 10 inches from the top of the posts, wrap 5 feet of wire around the bundle several times. Twist and snip the wire ends.

Step 2: Form a Tepee
Working with a helper, space the posts evenly apart, forming a tepee.

BHG TEST GARDEN TIP

DWARF CLEMATIS

Dwarf clematis is an ideal lightweight vine for growing on small structures such as a bent-twig tepee. They also do well in containers or along decks and patios. For a knockout mix, plant two colors, such as blue and white, together.

Step 3: Add an Internal Ring

Insert the metal macrame ring inside the posts to about a third of the way up the form. Use wire to secure the ring in place temporarily. You'll remove the ring when you're done weaving, so don't snip the wire ends.

Step 4: Nail in Place

Trim eight willow rods to equal length. Nail the base of one rod to the inside of a post just above the metal ring.

Step 5: Weave the Willow

Weave the rod over and under the next two posts counterclockwise, leaving the end free. Nail another rod to the next post clockwise. Weave it over and under the next two posts counterclockwise, placing it just above the first rod. Leave the end free. Continue in this fashion until each post has a rod nailed to it. Repeat the weaving technique: One at a time, weave the rods over and under the next two posts counterclockwise until all the rods are woven.

Step 6: Weave Another Section

Weave eight more rods directly above this first section. No need for nails now; simply wedge rods between posts. Repeat the process 20 inches above the weaving, using 16 more rods. Finish by twisting the willow rods to form a ropelike strand. Twine the willow rope around the tower until you reach the top. Tuck the ends into the wrapped post tops.

Step 7: Cover the Top Wire

Conceal the top wire using a willow rod. Remove the metal ring spacer. Trim the post tops. Push the tower into the ground. Anchor it using a metal rod if desired.

HARVESTING WILLOW FOR PROJECTS

Willow grows in long, supple rods. You can make a variety of projects such as tutuers, waddle fences, and even furniture. Here's how to harvest willow.

STEP 1: LOCATE WILLOW
Willow grows in moist areas around rivers. Or you can grow your own to harvest for projects.

STEP 2: CUT WILLOW RODS
Using loppers, cut the willow at the base of the plant.

STEP 3: STRIP OFF LEAVES
Run your hand down the length of the willow rod and strip off the leaves.

Classic Trellis

Create a vertical garden by training a flowering vine up a trellis mounted against a wall.

Build a flower-smothered wall treatment that's beautiful, fragrant, and wildlife-enhancing. Use rot-resistant wood, such as cedar or pressure-treated pine, to give your trellis durability. Use exterior-grade stain or primer and paint to protect your trellis. Painting before you assemble pieces may spare you brushwork later.

Step 1: Cut the Posts
Begin by preparing the 1×4 posts. The posts used here are 96 inches long. The lower 30 inches of the posts will be below ground when the trellis is in place. Cut decorative grooves into the front faces of the posts using a table saw or circular saw with a rip guide.

Step 2: Cut the Rails
Cut the rails to span the width of the trellis. This project is 19 inches wide. To make a similar trellis, cut two 19-inch-long rails from a 1×4. Rip the upper rail to 2½ inches wide.

Step 3: Prepare the Caps
Cut a 2×4 to span the width of the trellis plus 4 inches to create a pleasing overhang. The trellis here is 19 inches wide. To make a similar trellis, cut two 2×4s 23 inches long. One section will serve as the upper cap and the other will serve as a lower cap. Notch the 2×4s with a jigsaw to accommodate the posts. Cut additional decorative upper and lower caps using 1×4s or 2×4s as you see fit.

Step 4: Assemble the Structure
Assemble the posts, rails, and caps, fastening the wood with weatherproof glue and deck screws. The upper and lower rails are approximately 52 inches apart.

Step 5: Add the Wire
Place the trellis facedown. Partially drive ½-inch roofing nails around the perimeter of the opening every 4 inches. Secure a wire end to an upper-rail nail; loop the wire end twice around the nail, then wrap it around itself to secure. String the wire to a nail in the lower cap. Pull the wire taut enough to straighten it. Loop the wire once or twice around the nail and string the wire back up to the next nail on the upper rail. Continue for all the vertical wires. Repeat the process for the horizontal wires.

Step 6: Set the Trellis
Dig 30-inch-deep postholes and fill the bottom 6 inches of the holes with gravel. Place the trellis posts in the holes and plumb them. Backfill with soil and tamp to ensure the posts are stable.

Step 7: Plant Vines
Plant vining annuals, perennials, or shrubs at the base of the structure. Morning glory, black-eyed Susan vine, and sweet peas are easy to grow.

Time Required
1 to 2 days

Supplies Needed
Three 1×4s (8 feet long)
Circular saw or table saw
Two 2×4s (25 inches long)
Exterior-grade wood glue
8×1¼-inch deck screws
Roofing nails
30 feet of 14-gauge solid bare copper electrical wire
Posthole digger
Shovel
Gravel
Vining plants

START MORNING GLORY SEEDS

One of the best annual vines, morning glory blooms in shades of blue, pink, white, and red. It's earned its common name because the flowers tend to close by noon, especially in hot weather. Morning glory seeds are protected by a tough coat. Soak the seeds in water for 12–24 hours before sowing or file away or nick off a small piece of the coat before planting. Sow seeds ¼ inch deep; they usually sprout in about a week.

Time Required

1 to 2 days

Supplies Needed

Old window or door frame
Hammer
Nails
1×2s (optional)
Power drill/driver
Wooden fence posts
Tape measure
Marker
3-inch drywall screws
Screw eyes
20-gauge galvanized wire
Wire cutters
Seeds for climbing annuals

Door-Frame Trellis

Turn a vintage door frame or old window into a rustic trellis for vines. It's the ideal project for a cottage or country garden. Best of all, the more rustic, the better. No worries about painting (which is difficult once the structure is covered in vines).

Step 1: Brace the frame. Move your window frame to a work surface that is level and accessible from all sides. If you use architectural salvage for the frame, consider reinforcing it. Brace the frame by nailing 1×2s over all the joints and possibly along the entire length of the back. This frame was three-sided to begin with; nailing a 1×4 across the bottom strengthened the structure.

Step 2: Insert screw eyes. Starting at the top of the frame and working down, measure and mark 6-inch increments along the inside edge of the frame. These are the points where you'll insert screw eyes. Do this on all four sides of the frame. Predrill pilot holes at each mark, then twist the screw eyes into place.

Step 3: Add wire. Position vertical wires first by looping wire through the first screw eye at the top left. Twist the wire to secure it, then pull it taut to the corresponding eye at the bottom. Add 10 inches to the wire's length; clip, then twist the excess length to secure it. Repeat the process until all vertical wires are in place. To create horizontal rows, start at one side and weave wire over and under vertical rows to the opposite eye. Secure the wire ends.

opposite Morning glories are up to the challenge of scrambling long distances. Plant seeds or seedlings at the base of a structure and stand back. They grow quickly but will die back at frost, so you can try a new color next year.

Metal Arbor

Frame a walkway or make an entrance to an outdoor room with this graceful metal arbor.

Time Required

1 to 2 days

Supplies Needed

Wire cutters and protective gloves
Eight 10-foot lengths of rebar
Masking tape
Seventy-two 8- to 10-inch lengths of bare copper wire
Seventeen 4-foot lengths of rebar

BHG TEST GARDEN TIP

REBAR TIPS

Rebar, aka reinforcing bar, is a mesh of steel commonly used to reinforce concrete. This adaptable material can be used for a variety of gardening purposes. It makes ideal arbors because it can bend. Use sections of rebar in trellises for climbing vines. It can even be attached to a vertical surface, such as a garage side, to train plants on or against.

Step 1: Measure and Bend Rebar

Measure in 2 feet from one end of each 10-foot length of rebar. Mark the spot with masking tape. Bend each piece of rebar around a tree trunk at the 2-foot mark to form a partial arch. Push two rebar lengths at least 1 foot into the ground opposite each other. The arched ends should slightly overlap at the top.

Step 2: Bind the Ends

Bind the overlapping ends together with a piece of wire. Repeat with the remaining lengths of rebar, spacing the four resulting arches about 15 inches apart.

Step 3: Form the Cross Bars

Use the 4-foot lengths of rebar to form horizontal cross bars. Space them an equal distance apart and secure rebar with a piece of wire wherever two bars cross.

Step 4: Add Lighting

Attach hanging decorations, such as a Ball-jar lantern, to the arches as desired. The arbor will naturally weather to a rusty color.

CHAPTER SIX

Landscape Beauties

Transform your yard into an outdoor haven filled with gardening elements that reflect your personality and lifestyle.

Hose Hider

This custom structure turns a typical problem spot (how do you store a hose?) into a pretty garden feature. Inspired by garden picket fences, this hose hider works with any hanger that fastens to a wall. Attach it to the house or let it stand when you need it.

Time Required

2 to 4 hours

Supplies Needed

Seven 1×3 pine boards, 6 feet long
Circular saw
Pencil
36-ounce coffee can
Jigsaw
Clamps
Orbital sander
120-grit sandpaper
Speed square
Tape measure
Two 1×2 pine boards, 8 feet long
Wood glue
Drill bit (⁷⁄₆₄ inch)
Drill
One box containing 100 1¼-inch screws
One 1×8 pine board, 8 feet long
Safety glasses
Dust mask
Gate handle
Gate catch
Two hinges
Hose hanger

right Keep your garden hose neat and tidy (and out of view) with this attractive hose hider. Paint it to match the trim on your house for a custom look.

Step 1: Build the Sides

For the sides of the hose hider, use a circular saw to cut four 1×3s in half to create eight 3-foot-long boards. Using the top of the 36-ounce coffee can, trace a quarter-circle along a top corner of each cut board. Cut along the lines with a jigsaw to round off the boards. Save the cut pieces.

With the boards on edge and square at the bottom, clamp them all together. Sand circle cuts smooth.

Lay four of the sanded boards flat on your work surface to create the desired pattern, with any defects up. Using the scrap pieces as ¾-inch spacers, align the boards so that their tops create two half-circles. Repeat with the remaining 1×3 boards for the other side of the hose hider. Mark a line across each set of boards 2 inches from the bottom and another line 32 inches up.

From the 1×2s, cut four 12⅜-inch-long pieces. Align the top edge of one 1×2 piece along the bottom line marked for each set of side boards, leaving ½ inch along the bottom. Clamp into place and attach to the side boards with glue and two 1¼-inch screws per board. Countersink the screws. Make sure all boards remain properly aligned as you work. Attach 1×2s to the top of the side boards in the same manner, leaving 4 inches at the top. Remove spacers.

Step 2: Mount the Sides

Cut two 19½-inch-long pieces from the 1×8. Mark a line 9¾ inches in from a short edge of one. Mark this board "top."

Place the side pieces parallel to each other. Attach the top board, with the centerline facing down, flush with the edges of the sides and flush with the tops of the 1×2s. Glue and attach with six screws.

Attach the other 1×8 to the bottom. Make sure the bottoms of the 1×8 and the 1×2s are flush.

Step 3: Build the Door

Cut three 1×3s in half to create six 3-foot-long boards. Round the ends.

Cut two 18-inch lengths of 1×2. With the bad sides up, lay out the six 1×3s to create three half-circle peaks. Mark a line across all boards 3 inches from the bottom and another line 30 inches up.

Mark ¾ inch in on the outer boards. Align the bottom edge of one 18-inch-long 1×2 along the line 3 inches from the bottom, making sure ends are aligned with the ¾-inch marks. Affix using glue and 1¼-inch screws to attach the 1×2 to the two outer door boards. Clamp the 1×2 into place and attach to the door boards with glue and two 1¼-inch screws per board. Countersink the screws. Attach the top 1×2 brace the same way, with the top edge of the 1×2 aligned with the top line.

Attach the remaining 1×3 door boards in the same manner, spacing them about ⅞ inch apart.

Step 4: Make the Bottom Shelf

Cut an 18-inch piece from the remaining 1×8. Cut an 18-inch piece from the remaining 1×2. Attach it to the bottom shelf using glue and 1¼-inch screws, making sure the bottom of the 1×2 backer is flush with the shelf bottom.

With the backer board facing the back, install the bottom shelf inside the unit, resting it atop the bottom side braces and setting it back ¾ inch from the front. Two screws per side will suffice. When you drill the screws, be careful not to hit a screw on the bottom braces.

Install the 2-inch hinges on the edge of the door, 3 inches and 29 inches from the bottom. Install hinges on either the left or right side. Install the door on the case. Attach the handle, the catch, and the hose hanger.

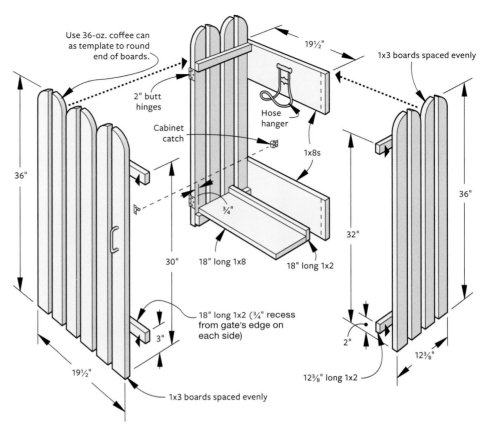

Use 36-oz. coffee can as template to round end of boards.

2" butt hinges

Cabinet catch

Hose hanger

1x3 boards spaced evenly

19½"

1x8s

36"

36"

32"

30"

18" long 1x8

18" long 1x2

¾"

18" long 1x2 (¾" recess from gate's edge on each side)

3"

2"

12⅜"

12⅜" long 1x2

19½"

1x3 boards spaced evenly

Cool Cold Frame

Use a discarded window and old garden tools to craft an ideal tool for hardening off plants.

Time Required

1 to 2 days

Supplies Needed

Salvaged window frame

2×8 boards

Hinges

Vintage garden hand tools

Antique table legs

Wire edging

Make a cold frame for your garden to harden off spring plants and prolong the harvest season in the fall. With an old window frame, some scrap wood, and other finds from the garden shed, you can make a cold frame as individual as you are.

Step 1: Find an Old Window
If one isn't available, try a new barn sash from a farm store.

Step 2: Build the Box
Size the box to fit the window frame. Make it taller in the back to accommodate taller plants.

Step 3: Add Hinges
A couple of hinges on the back allow you to prop open the window frame on hot days.

Step 4: Install Finials
Fashion finials from old garden tools and sawed-off pieces of table legs. Add a decorative trim of wire for good looks.

Flower Wall

A bevy of brightly painted terra-cotta pots makes a beautiful vertical fencescape.

Time Required

2 to 4 hours

Supplies Needed

9 same-size terra-cotta pots

Enamel spray paint in aqua and lime green

Tape

9 pot clips

3 pink petunia plants

3 'Diamond Frost' euphorbia

3 'Marguerite' sweet potato vine

Potting soil

Hang up a group of shiny pots packed with a bounty of blooms. This simple planting scheme dresses up a blank fence or the side of a garage. Choose sun-loving plants for sunny spots and shade-loving plants for areas with lower light.

Step 1: Spray-Paint Pots
Tape the terra-cotta rims, then spray-paint each pot. Allow the pots to dry. Remove the tape from the rims.

Step 2: Plant the Flowers
Fill each pot with potting soil and plants.

Step 3: Install Pot Clips
Attach a pot clip onto the fence or wall for each container.

Step 4: Hang Up Pots
Insert the rim into the pot clip and slide it forward to rest on the base of the clip. Water plants as the soil dries out.

Magical Landscape

Transform a large tray and a collection of small-scale plants into an enchanted landscape. From the teeny-tiny glass house to itty-bitty tools and thimble-size pots, the design works as a study in detail.

Time Required

2 to 4 hours

Supplies Needed

13×30×2-inch metal boot tray

Hammer

Awl or large nail

Pea gravel

Coarse sand

Potting mix

Tabletop terrarium

Miniature fountain, fencing, benches, garden tools, and pots

Aquarium gravel

Plant stand

Sawara cypress (*Chamaecyparis pisifera* 'Cannon Ball')

Thrift (*Armeria* spp.)

Hens-and-chicks (*Sempervivum* 'Sanford Hybrid' and 'Cobweb')

Alpine white spruce (*Picea glauca* 'Witches Broom')

Stonecrop pink spurium (*Sedum coccineum*)

Stonecrop (*Sedum makinoi* 'Ogon')

Dwarf wintercreeper (*Euonymus* 'Kewensis')

Bronze Dutch clover (*Trifolium repens* 'Atropurpureum')

Dwarf Canadian hemlock (*Tsuga Canadensis* 'Burkett's White Tip')

Tabletop gardens typically combine a shallow container with petite plants or dwarf varieties and, if you like, other pipsqueak features—a miniature gazebo, pebbled path, and decorative doodads —to make an enchanting scene that rewards curiosity.

Step 1: Make Drainage Holes

Using a hammer and awl or large nail, poke holes for drainage about every 6 inches in the bottom of the metal tray.

Step 2: Add Gravel, Sand, and Potting Mix

Cover the bottom of the tray with a ½-inch-deep layer of 2 parts pea gravel and 1 part coarse sand. Top with a layer of potting mix, mounding it at least 2 inches deep.

Step 3: Add Small Plants

Add plants, beginning with the largest specimens (dwarf conifers and succulents) and filling in with alpines and groundcovers. When planting, gently loosen root balls and shake loose extraneous soil, if necessary, to tuck the roots into the potting mix. Leave room for pathways and your selection of miniature features, such as a glass house (tabletop terrarium), fountain, and other accessories.

Step 4: Sprinkle Gravel

With the plants and furnishings in place, sprinkle aquarium gravel over any exposed potting mix to prevent erosion.

Step 5: Water Thoroughly

Water well after planting; thereafter, water only when the potting mix feels dry.

Step 6: Display and Enjoy

Place the garden in a lightly shaded area where it will not bake in the sun. In cold climates, move the tray indoors for winter. A cool room with bright light is best.

Time Required

2 to 4 hours

Supplies Needed

Concrete birdbath (with separate basin and pedestal)

Pea gravel

Moisture-retentive crystals

Potting mix (that contains fertilizer)

Geodes and decorative stones

Decorative mushrooms and other ornaments

Log moss (*Neckera complanata*), in the center

Clover (*Trifolium* spp.), on the left

Club moss/trailing spikemoss (*Selaginella kraussiana*), on the top right

Fairy Garden

Escape into a lush and tranquil realm, reminiscent of a forest floor, where mosses flourish and mushrooms sprout.

Imagine an idyllic landscape filled with moss, geodes, and tiny creatures. That's the fun little fairy garden you can make in the top of a cast-off birdbath or basin. It's easy to build a well-drained base (the pea gravel helps with that). Then top with potting mix and plant velvety moss and little plants of clover. Add the magical elements that you like: ceramic mushrooms, smooth or craggy stones, and other treasures. This is an ideal project for kids, who will love to change out the elements.

Step 1: Add Pea Gravel
Cover the bottom of the birdbath basin with a 1-inch layer of pea gravel.

Step 2: Add Potting Mix
Blend moisture-retentive crystals with potting mix according to package directions. Fill the basin with potting mix, mounding it up to 4 inches above the rim.

Step 3: Add Log Moss
Cover the mound with a blanket of fresh log moss and a sprig of clover if desired. Leave room to plant the club moss (or trailing spikemoss).

Step 4: Add Decorations
Place decorative rocks, ornamental mushrooms, and other natural-looking accents here and there, nestling them into the moss so they won't tumble out.

Step 5: Use Club Moss
Use club moss as an accent planting, positioning it behind the large geode. Water regularly. Shower the garden regularly to keep it moist, green, and lush.

Table Garden

Use groundcovers to create an astonishingly lush tabletop. Creeping groundcovers form a flat, firm surface, while sprawling plants spill over the edges. In about a month, five 4-inch plants, split up for planting in a pattern, will cover a 21-inch-diameter tabletop.

Time Required

2 to 4 hours

Supplies Needed

Steel-wire plant table

Landscaping fabric

Moisture-retentive crystals

Potting mix

Log moss

Corsican mint (*Mentha requienii*)

Prostrate peppermint (*Mentha piperita*)

Gold Scotch moss (*Sagina subulata* 'Aurea')

Maiden pinks (*Dianthus deltoides* 'Brilliant')

Step 1: Add Landscape Fabric
Line the tabletop with landscaping fabric, tucking and folding it to fit.

Step 2: Add Potting Mix
Blend moisture-retentive crystals with potting mix according to package directions. Fill the tabletop with potting mix.

Step 3: Use Log Moss
Tuck the log moss in between the tabletop and the landscape fabric to camouflage the fabric and give the table a softer appearance.

Step 4: Plant the Tabletop
Nestle the other plants into the potting mix, planting at the same level they grew in their nursery pots.

Step 5: Set in Sun
Situate the table in a sunny place. Water thoroughly and regularly to keep the soil moist. Trim sprawlers regularly to keep them growing low and lush.

COLD-WEATHER CARE

If you live in a cold-climate region, lift the plants out of the tabletop in early fall and transplant them into the garden. That way they'll provide you with divisions for replanting in spring.

A low-growing tabletop of herbs and mosses makes a beautiful focal point on a patio or in a garden bed.

Hypertufa Trough

Show off your favorite container plants in a homemade hypertufa trough. Modeled after ancient stone troughs used to hold water and feed for livestock, these troughs are made from hypertufa, an artificial stone product. Once you learn the secret to making these containers, you may not want to stop. Our plan makes a 16×16-inch trough.

Time Required

1 to 2 days

Supplies Needed

Serrated knife

Sheet of 2-inch-thick foam insulation board

Eight 3¼-inch nails

Tape

Tape measure or ruler

Marker

Rubber or latex gloves

Quikrete portland cement

Perlite

Peat moss

Reinforced concrete fibers

Water

Gallon container

½-inch dowel

⅜-inch-thick plywood board (2×2 feet)

Spray bottle

Sheet of plastic or trash bag

Wire brush or screwdriver (optional)

Wheelbarrow

Hoe

Step 1: Prepare the Mold

Using the serrated knife, cut insulation into two 16×6-inch pieces and two 18×6-inch pieces. Assemble these four sections into a square or rectangle, depending on how you join the ends. For a rectangle, assemble as shown with the 16-inch section outside the 18-inch section. For a square, assemble with the 16-inch section inside the 18-inch section. Insert two nails through the insulation material—one near the top and one near the bottom—of each intersection.

Step 2: Secure the Mold

Wrap tape two times around the mold, once near the top and once near the bottom, for added reinforcement. Almost any type of tape will work: duct tape, masking tape, or painter's tape.

Step 3: Mark a Thickness Line

Mark a line at least 2 inches from the bottom as a guide to the depth of the hypertufa; this will mark the thickness of the bottom of your trough. If you create a larger container, you'll want a deeper layer of hypertufa to give your trough more support.

opposite Lightweight hypertufa is easy to make in a variety of shapes.

Hypertufa Trough

Step 4: Mix the Dry Materials

Put on your gloves and measure 2 gallons cement, 2 gallons perlite, and 4 gallons peat moss. The amount will allow for some leftover material to make trough feet. Mix the dry ingredients in your wheelbarrow with the hoe.

To give your hypertufa trough more strength, add ⅓ cup reinforced concrete fibers. Find them at building supply stores.

Step 5: Add Water

Slowly add warm water to the wheelbarrow. Start with about 3 gallons and mix it well with the dry materials. You should end up with a consistency like cookie dough or graham cracker crust. It should be wet enough to hold together when compressed, but not oozing water.

Step 6: Form the Trough

Set the mold on the plywood board. Begin packing the bottom with the hypertufa mixture, using your previously marked line as a stopping point. Working a small area at a time, use your hands to firmly press the mixture into the bottom corners and up the sides, making sure to mash one section into another for seamless adhesion for a strong trough. Continue up the sides until they are covered by a 2-inch-thick layer. Spray water as needed to keep the mixture moist while you are working. The plywood board serves as the bottom of the mold and makes transporting the trough easier.

Step 7: Add Drainage Holes
To provide proper drainage, use a dowel to poke holes in the bottom of the trough. Insert the dowel through the hypertufa until it meets the plywood base. Repeat to make six evenly spaced holes. Leave the trough to dry in a protected spot.

Step 8: Remove the Mold
Your trough should dry in about 48 hours. After it has dried and hardened, carefully remove the tape and nails and pull the sides of the mold away from the trough. The trough can be used as is. Or if you prefer a textured, aged look for your trough, gently score the exterior with a wire brush or screwdriver.

Step 9: Cure the Trough
Store the trough in a shady area to cure for 30–60 days. The hypertufa trough gets stronger every day. Your container can be left out in freezing temperatures as long as it is off the ground. Spraying with water often decreases the duration of this process to about 30 days.

MAKE POT FEET
Use any leftover mixture to create feet to keep your trough off the ground.

Garden Bench Planter

A super seating area for a small space, this citrus-orange bench also features an inset planter for small shrubs. Use a vintage paneled wood door as the base.

Time Required

2 to 4 hours

Supplies Needed

Solid-wood door with horizontal paneled sections

Sawhorses or workbench

Drill with a ¾-inch spade bit

Saber saw

Pliers

Wood glue

Wood strips

1×3-inch wood boards for edging (we used poplar)

2-inch stainless-steel screws

Sandpaper

Exterior primer and paint

Two planter boxes (select planters that can bear the weight of a person on the bench and are sized to fit inside the panel openings)

Potting soil

Two shrubs or other container-loving plants

Step 1: Drill a Hole in the Panel
Place the door on sawhorses or a workbench. Position the drill bit about ¾ inch inside the edge of one of the door's end panels. Drill a hole into the panel.

Step 2: Cut Out the Panel
Insert the blade of the saber saw into the hole and cut out the panel. Be sure to hold the panel securely as you complete your cut to ensure the wood does not splinter.

opposite A bright orange bench (with built-in greenery) offers inviting seating and a stunning focal point to a small yard or corner.

Garden Bench Planter

Step 3: Remove Excess Pieces
Use pliers to remove any excess wood from the door.

Step 4: Fill In Gaps
To fill any gaps or visible channels in the door, use wood glue to adhere strips of wood cut to fit.

Step 6: Add Reinforcement
To reinforce the door, cut 1×3-inch wood boards with the saber saw to the door's measurements, allowing extra to butt at the corners. Screw the boards to the door and to each other. If you don't want the screw holes to show, fill them with wood putty.

Step 5: Frame the Hole
Insert wood strips into visible channels. If needed, pound in with a hammer. Repeat the preceding steps on the panel on the other end of the door.

Step 7: Sand, Paint, and Add Soil
Sand the door and apply one coat of an exterior primer; let dry. Paint the entire piece with a high-quality exterior paint; let dry. Place the door so openings align with planters positioned underneath. Fill the planters with soil and shrubs.

Outdoor Room

Grow an open-air pavilion. Four plum trees define this rustic backyard getaway atop a pea-gravel patio. The trees' twining branches will fill in to cover the supports. In three to five years, after the branches intertwine sufficiently, you'll be able to remove the stakes and supports.

Time Required

2 to 4 hours

Supplies Needed

4 9-foot-tall plum trees

Landscape cloth

7 bags of pea gravel

4 9-foot-tall red-oak stakes

8 6-foot lengths of bamboo

2½-inch galvanized decking
    screws

Garden twine

Pruners

Spade

Step 1: Make the Pad

Mow a 6×6-foot grassy area very short. Plant a young, 9-foot-tall plum tree at each of the four corners. Place gray landscape cloth over the square and cover it with pea gravel a few inches thick.

Step 2: Build the Structure

Prune the lower branches. Pound a 9-foot red-oak stake about a foot into the ground next to each of the four trees. Using 6-foot lengths of bamboo, form two 6×6-foot squares, lashing the corners of each square together with twine. Insert a 2½-inch galvanized decking screw about ¾ inch into the outside of each oak stake, 11 inches below the top. Slide one bamboo square over the stakes so it rests on the screws.

Step 3: Create the Canopy

Insert a 2½-inch decking screw about ¾ inch into the outside of each oak stake, 3 inches below the top. Slide the other bamboo square over the stakes so it rests on the top set of screws. To secure the squares, lash the bamboo to the stakes with twine. Remove all but the top four branches of each tree. Bend two of the top four branches to the left. Use twine to tie one branch to the top bamboo support and the other to the bottom.

Step 4: Tie in Place

Bend the remaining two branches of each tree to the right, using twine to tie them to the squares in the same way as in Step 3.

Mosaic Walkway

Turn a section of a walkway into a fantastic focal point by crafting a pebble mosaic. Use smooth stones to make your own design.

Transform an entryway path into a textural masterpiece with an artistic mosaic of pebbles and stones. You can create your own design, depending on the size of stones you use, or follow the easy-to-assemble design here.

Time Required

1 to 2 days

Supplies Needed

Pebbles and stones of different sizes
Sand
Water
Level
Rubber-headed mallet
Leaf blower
Garden hose
Spray mister
Broom
Sponge

Step 1: Size Pebbles
Sort pebbles by size, choosing flat ovals, *right*, rather than irregular shapes.

Step 2: Build a Sand Bed
Fill a framed concrete base with a thin layer of slightly moist sand mix. Arrange the pebbles into the desired pattern and tap into place.

Step 3: Level Up
Use a level to make sure pebble surface is even with adjacent walkways and will drain away from the mosaic's center.

Step 4: Add More Rows
Repeat Steps 2 and 3 for adjacent rows of pebbles. If desired, include special stones as focal points.

opposite A mosaic walkway is a beautiful addition to any front entry. You don't need a large space to make a big impression.

Step 5: Make Adjustments
While sand mix is still moist, make final adjustments to the pebbles with light taps of a rubber mallet.

Step 6: Remove Sand
Gently blow excess sand mix from the mosaic using a leaf blower on low idle. Then dampen with a spray mister attachment on a garden hose.

Step 8: Moisten Mosaic
Squeeze water from a sponge over the mosaic. Mist once a day for five days to give it time to set. Avoid walking on it for a week.

Step 7: Sit and Settle
Let stand for 2 hours. Softly add and brush in moist sand mix between the pebbles to grout. This creates a finished surface.

BHG TEST GARDEN TIP · OTHER NATURAL PATHWAYS

Stone is a long-lasting paving option. Here are options from small to large:

PEA GRAVEL This small stone is easy to install. Just dump it into the space and rake it into place. It needs an edged area so it doesn't spill into the lawn.

CRUSHED STONE Larger and more angular than pea gravel, crushed stone works well as a pathway. You can get it in many colors to match your landscape.

FLAGSTONE Large stones set into the ground offer sure footing and little care. Soften their look by planting moss or treadable herbs between the cracks.

Fire Pit

Keep the outdoor entertaining going long into the night and well after summer is over.

A fire pit is a warm and wonderful way to enjoy your patio after the sun has gone down. A glowing fire extends the use of your patio, warming up cool spring and autumn nights.

You can add a metal insert (like the photo *below*). Or you can simply build the pit with stones (like the project *opposite*). Before installing an open fire pit, check local regulations. Local codes often outline siting specifications and may require you to apply for a recreational-burning permit. In some locations, any sort of open fire is illegal.

Time Required

1 to 2 days

Supplies Needed

Stake

String

Spray paint

Shovel

Gravel

Sand

Rake

Tamping tool

Level

Small, curved, modular
   retaining-wall blocks

Concrete adhesive

Rubber-headed mallet

Step 1: Find a Flat Spot
Start by finding a flat area 10–12 feet in diameter. Use a stake, string, and spray paint to draw the perimeter of the pit. (Before you start digging, lay out your blocks to determine the diameter of the pit.) Dig out dirt within the marked circle; ours is 56 inches in diameter and 18 inches deep.

Step 2: Add Gravel
Fill the pit with 6 inches of gravel; rake smooth and tamp after each load to ensure a solid base. Then spread a thin layer of coarse sand over the gravel. Tamp the sand as well and make sure the surface is level.

Step 3: Make the Surround
To create the fire pit surround, use small, curved, modular retaining-wall blocks. Use string and spray paint to mark an inner circle as a guideline for placing the first layer of retaining-wall blocks. (We used a 38-inch inner diameter.)

Step 4: Set the First Row
Place the first row of retaining-wall blocks in a complete circle, securing them into the gravel and sand base with a mallet. Use a level to make sure the blocks are level from side to side and front to back.

Step 5: Stack the Second Level
Add a second row of retaining-wall blocks. Look for interlocking blocks to simplify this step. Add the top row of coping blocks. Use a concrete adhesive to glue these into place.

Bamboo Planter

This tropical-style plant stand goes together easily using off-the-shelf materials readily available from home improvement centers. Change the look of your garden anytime you want. Simply drop pots from the garden center directly into the planter. No digging, no transplanting.

Here's the perfect container garden for gardeners with little space—and little time for digging and transplanting. This stylish bamboo structure is more of a plant showcase than garden. The base is created so you can slip in pots of plants without digging or transplanting. You'll never get your hands dirty!

This bamboo beauty is an ideal place to summer your indoor houseplants. Or create a quick garden by buying several pots of cool-weather annuals, such as pansies. When the weather warms up, change out the pansies for hot-weather beauties such as petunias or geraniums. You can even plant a veggie and herb garden in pots—just drop them in and you are done.

Tools

Saw (handsaw, saber saw, or circular saw)

Electric drill

Drill bits

Hammer

Screwdriver (or screwdriver bit for electric drill)

Tape measure

2- to 3-inch synthetic bristle paintbrush

Minimum of two 6-inch C-clamps (or a helper)

Awl (or a large nail)

Time Required

6 to 8 hours

Materials

One 3-inch-diameter wood fence post

Two 8-foot-long 1×8 cedar boards (sanded on one side)

One piece 4×4×½-inch water-resistant plywood (marine plywood shown; treated plywood also acceptable)

Six 2-inch-diameter bamboo posts (lengths shown: four 44 inches, two 54 inches)

8 feet ready-made bamboo edging for sides (graduated edging shown is 8–12 inches high)

6 feet fencing/edging for front (10-inch split bamboo shown was cut from 36-inch fence)

6-foot, ½-inch-diameter bamboo rod

50-foot roll of 19-gauge dark annealed steel wire

100 feet of natural sisal cord

100 feet of ¼-inch twine

1 quart exterior primer

1 quart exterior latex paint in color to suit (color shown echoes natural bamboo)

Polished stones (or red lava rock)

18 #10×2½-inch stainless-steel flathead wood screws

Small box stainless-steel 1¼-inch common nails (used for siding trim)

Small box #8×1¼-inch exterior flathead wood screws

Six 6-inch landscape-timber screws

right Give your indoor houseplants a summer vacation by simply dropping them into this bamboo planter.

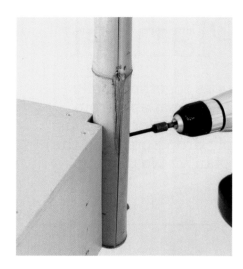

Step 1: Cut and Attach Legs

Cut three 12-inch legs from fence post. From 1×8 boards, cut front to chosen length; then cut sides to form a right triangle (sides shown are 37¾ inches each, with a 53⅜-inch front). With clamps, position boards against legs so all boards meet in a V. Hold tops of side boards even with top of corner leg; attach each side board to leg with three #10×2½-inch screws. Using the same fasteners and alignment, attach front board and sides to two front legs.

Step 2: Build the Base

Cut plywood top flush with outer edge of base (40⅝×40⅝×57½ inches shown). Notch plywood to follow V joints (see "Snug It In" *below*). Attach top with #8×1¼-inch screws every 8 inches. Apply primer and two coats exterior paint. With 2-inch bamboo uprights sitting in V joints, mark and drill two ¼-inch-diameter holes through uprights with holes centered over each leg. Drive two landscape screws through holes in each leg.

Step 3: Add Edging

Attach edging along two sides. (We used a commercial off-the-shelf product.) Edging shown is stretched taut and attached to bamboo uprights with steel wire; hide wire with sisal cord for appearance of traditional lashing. Front shown is covered with split-bamboo fencing cut from a 36-inch-high roll. The 10-inch height shown extends 2 inches above plywood platform to contain polished stones. Fencing, attached with galvanized staples, rests on ½-inch-diameter bamboo rod attached with stainless-steel nails driven through predrilled holes to prevent splitting.

SNUG IT IN

Small steps can make a big difference. Once the plywood top is attached, cut the corners (A) to accommodate the notch created by the intersecting base boards. This creates a cradle (B) for the bamboo uprights, resulting in a tighter fit and more stability.

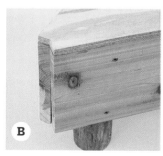

Step 4: Add Bamboo Supports

Drill one ⅛-inch-diameter hole completely through each bamboo upright 6 inches from top. Run wire through holes to attach and support horizontal poles. Conceal wire with twine lashings. Cut holes so rims of pots rest on plywood base (5¾-inch-diameter and 8-inch-diameter shown). Insert potted plants. To fill in the blanks around the pots, add moss, mulch, or stones.

Plant List

A. Corn Plant
  (*Dracaena*)

B. Croton
  (*Codiaeum variegatum pictum*)

C. Dumb Cane
  (*Dieffenbachia*)

D. Variegated Swedish Ivy
  (*Plectranthus verticillatus*)

Corn Plant

Croton

Dumb Cane

Swedish Ivy

USDA Plant Hardiness Zone Map

Each plant has an ability to withstand low temperatures. This range of temperatures is expressed as a Zone—and a Zone map shows where you can grow a plant.

Planting for your Zone

The U.S. Department of Agriculture designates 11 Zones from Canada to Mexico, and each represents the lowest expected winter temperature in that area. Each Zone is based on a 10°F difference in minimum temperatures. Once you know your hardiness Zone, you can choose plants for your garden that will flourish. Look for the hardiness Zone on the plant tags of the perennials, trees, and shrubs you buy.

Microclimates in your yard

Not all areas in your yard are the same. Depending on geography, trees, and structures, some spots may receive different sunlight and wind and consequently experience temperature differences. Take a look around your yard; you may notice that the same plant comes up sooner in one place than another. This is the microclimate concept in action. A microclimate is an area in your yard that is slightly different (cooler or warmer) than the other areas of your yard.

Create a microclimate

Once you're aware of your yard's microclimates, use them to your advantage. For example, you may be able to grow plants in a sheltered, south-facing garden bed that you can't grow elsewhere in your yard. You can create a microclimate by planting evergreens on the north side of a property to block prevailing winds. Or plant deciduous trees on the south side to provide shade in summer.

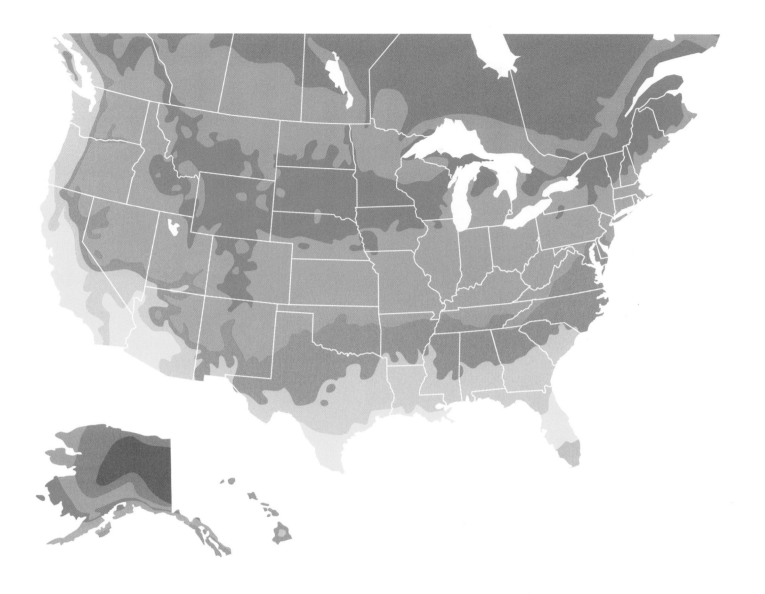

Source: U.S. Department of Agriculture

Range of Average Annual Minimum Temperatures for Each Zone

- Zone 1: below -50°F (below -45.6°C)
- Zone 2: -50 to -40°F (-45 to -40°C)
- Zone 3: -40 to -30°F (-40 to -35°C)
- Zone 4: -30 to -20°F (-34 to -29°C)

- Zone 5: -20 to -10°F (-29 to -23°C)
- Zone 6: -10 to 0°F (-23 to -18°C)
- Zone 7: 0 to 10°F (-18 to -12°C)
- Zone 8: 10 to 20°F (-12 to -7°C)

- Zone 9: 20 to 30°F (-7 to -1°C)
- Zone 10: 30 to 40°F (-1 to 4°C)
- Zone 11: 40°F and above (4.5°C and above)

opposite Spring gardens are awash in blue blooms. Iris, chives, and catmint are all early-spring perennial flowers.

Index